WORLD EXPLORERS

Alexander von Humboldt
Colossus of Exploration

Ann Gaines

CHELSEA HOUSE PUBLISHERS

New York · Philadelphia

On the cover   Map of South America featuring the Amazon
River and its tributaries. Humboldt portrait in inset.

Chelsea House Publishers
Editor-in-Chief   Remmel Nunn
Managing Editor   Karyn Gullen Browne
Copy Chief   Juliann Barbato
Picture Editor   Adrian G. Allen
Art Director   Maria Epes
Deputy Copy Chief   Mark Rifkin
Assistant Art Director   Noreen Romano
Manufacturing Manager   Gerald Levine
Systems Manager   Lindsey Ottman
Production Manager   Joseph Romano
Production Coordinator   Marie Claire Cebrián

World Explorers
Senior Editor   Sean Dolan

Staff for ALEXANDER VON HUMBOLDT, COLOSSUS OF EXPLORATION
Associate Editor   Terrance Dolan
Copy Editor   Philip Koslow
Editorial Assistant   Martin Mooney
Picture Researcher   Diana Gongora
Senior Designer   Barbara Niemczyc

First Printing

1   3   5   7   9   8   6   4   2

Library of Congress Cataloging-in-Publication Data

Gaines, Ann.
Alexander von Humboldt, colossus of exploration/Ann Gaines.
p.   cm.—(World explorers)
Includes bibliographical references and index.
Summary: Examines the life and times of the German scientist and
geographer who helped found modern geography and pioneered in
plant geography and climatology.
ISBN 0-7910-1313-8
      0-7910-1537-8 (pbk.)
1. Humboldt, Alexander von, 1769–1859—Biography—Juvenile
literature.   2. Scientists—Germany—Biography—Juvenile literature.
3. Naturalists—Germany—Biography—Juvenile literature.
[1. Humboldt, Alexander von, 1769–1859.   2. Scientists.
3. Geographers.]   I. Title.   II. Series.
Q143.H9G36   1990
574'.092—dc20   90-2261
[B]   CIP
[92]   AC

Alexander von Humboldt
Colossus of Exploration

General Editor

William H. Goetzmann
Jack S. Blanton, Sr., Chair in History
   University of Texas at Austin

Consulting Editor

Tom D. Crouch
Chairman, Department of Aeronautics
   National Air and Space Museum
   Smithsonian Institution

CONTENTS

WORLD EXPLORERS

CHELSEA HOUSE PUBLISHERS

Into the Unknown

Michael Collins

It is difficult to define most eras in history with any precision, but not so the space age. On October 4, 1957, it burst on us with little warning when the Soviet Union launched *Sputnik*, a 184-pound cannonball that circled the globe once every 96 minutes. Less than 4 years later, the Soviets followed this first primitive satellite with the flight of Yuri Gagarin, a 27-year-old fighter pilot who became the first human to orbit the earth. The Soviet Union's success prompted President John F. Kennedy to decide that the United States should "land a man on the moon and return him safely to earth" before the end of the 1960s. We now had not only a space age but a space race.

I was born in 1930, exactly the right time to allow me to participate in Project Apollo, as the U.S. lunar program came to be known. As a young man growing up, I often found myself too young to do the things I wanted—or suddenly too old, as if someone had turned a switch at midnight. But for Apollo, 1930 was the perfect year to be born, and I was very lucky. In 1966 I enjoyed circling the earth for three days, and in 1969 I flew to the moon and laughed at the sight of the tiny earth, which I could cover with my thumbnail.

How the early explorers would have loved the view from space! With one glance Christopher Columbus could have plotted his course and reassured his crew that the world was indeed round. In 90 minutes Magellan could have looked down at every port of call in the *Victoria's* three-year circumnavigation of the globe. Given a chance to map their route from orbit, Lewis and Clark could have told President Jefferson that there was no easy Northwest Passage but that a continent of exquisite diversity awaited their scrutiny.

In a physical sense, we have already gone to most places that we can. That is not to say that there are not new adventures awaiting us deep in the sea or on the red plains of Mars, but more important than reaching new places will be understanding those we have already visited. There are vital gaps in our understanding of how our planet works as an ecosystem and how our planet fits into the infinite order of the universe. The next great age may well be the age of assimilation, in which we use microscope and telescope to evaluate what we have discovered and put that knowledge to use. The adventure of being first to reach may be replaced by the satisfaction of being first to grasp. Surely that is a form of exploration as vital to our well-being, and perhaps even survival, as the distinction of being the first to explore a specific geographical area.

The explorers whose stories are told in the books of this series did not just sail perilous seas, scale rugged mountains, traverse blistering deserts, dive to the depths of the ocean, or land on the moon. Their voyages and expeditions were journeys of mind as much as of time and distance, through which they—and all of mankind—were able to reach a greater understanding of our universe. That challenge remains, for all of us. The imperative is to see, to understand, to develop knowledge that others can use, to help nurture this planet that sustains us all. Perhaps being born in 1975 will be as lucky for a new generation of explorer as being born in 1930 was for Neil Armstrong, Buzz Aldrin, and Mike Collins.

The Reader's Journey

William H. Goetzmann

This volume is one of a series that takes us with the great explorers of the ages on bold journeys over the oceans and the continents and into outer space. As we travel along with these imaginative and courageous journeyers, we share their adventures and their knowledge. We also get a glimpse of that mysterious and inextinguishable fire that burned in the breast of men such as Magellan and Columbus—the fire that has propelled all those throughout the ages who have been driven to leave behind family and friends for a voyage into the unknown.

No one has ever satisfactorily explained the urge to explore, the drive to go to the "back of beyond." It is certain that it has been present in man almost since he began walking erect and first ventured across the African savannas. Sparks from that same fire fueled the transoceanic explorers of the Ice Age, who led their people across the vast plain that formed a land bridge between Asia and North America, and the astronauts and scientists who determined that man must reach the moon.

Besides an element of adventure, all exploration involves an element of mystery. We must not confuse exploration with discovery. Exploration is a purposeful human activity—a search for something. Discovery may be the end result of that search; it may also be an accident, as when Columbus found a whole new world while searching for the Indies. Often, the explorer may not even realize the full significance of what he has discovered, as was the case with Columbus. Exploration, on the other hand, is the product of a cultural or individual curiosity; it is a unique process that has enabled mankind to know and understand the world's oceans, continents, and polar regions. It is at the heart of scientific thinking. One of its most significant aspects is that it teaches people to ask the right questions; by doing so, it forces us to reevaluate what we think we know and understand. Thus knowledge progresses, and we are driven constantly to a new awareness and appreciation of the universe in all its infinite variety.

The motivation for exploration is not always pure. In his fascination with the new, man often forgets that others have been there before him. For example, the popular notion of the discovery of America overlooks the complex Indian civilizations that had existed there for thousands of years before the arrival of Europeans. Man's desire for conquest, riches, and fame is often linked inextricably with his quest for the unknown, but a story that touches so closely on the human essence must of necessity treat war as well as peace, avarice with generosity, both pride and humility, frailty and greatness. The story of exploration is above all a story of humanity and of man's understanding of his place in the universe.

The WORLD EXPLORERS series has been divided into four sections. The first treats the explorers of the ancient world, the Viking explorers of the 9th through the 11th centuries, and Marco Polo and the medieval explorers. The rest of the series is divided into three great ages of exploration. The first is the era of Columbus and Magellan: the period spanning the 15th and 16th centuries, which saw the discovery and exploration of the New World and the world ocean. The second might be called the age of science and imperialism, the era made possible by the scientific advances of the 17th century, which witnessed the discovery of the world's last two undiscovered continents, Australia and Antarctica, the mapping of all the continents and oceans, and the establishment of colonies all over the world. The third great age refers to the most ambitious quests of the 20th century—the probing of space and of the ocean's depths.

As we reach out into the darkness of outer space and other galaxies, we come to better understand how our ancestors confronted *oecumene*, or the vast earthly unknown. We learn once again the meaning of an unknown 18th-century sea captain's advice to navigators:

> And if by chance you make a landfall on the shores of another sea in a far country inhabited by savages and barbarians, remember you this: the greatest danger and the surest hope lies not with fires and arrows but in the quicksilver hearts of men.

At its core, exploration is a series of moral dramas. But it is these dramas, involving new lands, new people, and exotic ecosystems of staggering beauty, that make the explorers' stories not only moral tales but also some of the greatest adventure stories ever recorded. They represent the process of learning in its most expansive and vivid forms. We see that real life, past and present, transcends even the adventures of the starship *Enterprise*.

Unlimited Horizons

The news had begun to spread throughout Quito, a lively town nestled in Ecuador's portion of the great Andes mountain range, in mid-May: The strange European was going to climb—or attempt to climb—terrible Pichincha, a live volcano so tall that it wore clouds as a cloak. As the European strolled about the streets of Quito, trying in a pleasant manner to find an Indian who would accompany him on his climb, the townspeople gaped. His appearance in itself was enough to invite stares; the locals had never seen anyone like this before. He had a pale face, fair hair, blue eyes, a large, prominent nose, a high forehead, and an unusually good physique. Even stranger was his clothing—baggy striped trousers, a tall black hat, and high black boots with the toes curled over. He carried mysterious instruments and contraptions wherever he went. Some of the Indians thought he might be a sorcerer, and indeed he was in some ways a Faustian figure, a man who quite literally wanted to learn everything about everything. But the ally of this Faust was not the devil; it was science.

Now he announced that he was going to climb Pichincha. They all agreed that he was very brave—or very foolish. Pichincha would most likely swallow up this odd stranger, and he would never be seen again. Nevertheless, the European found a guide, a fearless and good-natured Indian named Aldas, and on May 26, 1802, they began their assault on smoldering Pichincha. The entire town

Scientist and explorer Alexander von Humboldt is tempted by Death, who invites him to exchange his life for complete knowledge of the cosmos. Like the legendary Faust, who sold his soul to the devil in exchange for universal knowledge, Humboldt burned to know everything.

turned out to see them off, and they watched as the 2 men made good time up the base of the 15,000-foot volcano. But soon the climbers disappeared into the mists that shrouded the volcano's upper reaches, and the townspeople went home, some of them shaking their head. A few were old enough to remember the last time a European—a Frenchman—had come to climb the volcano, some 60 years before. Pichincha had shrugged off the unfortunate fellow as if he were a flea, leaving him exhausted and frostbitten; he was lucky to have made it down alive.

Aldas and the European climbed steadily. It was a treacherous ascent. The lava-encrusted slopes were covered with ice, and the fog grew thicker and thicker; it was as if they were climbing into the heavens. As they neared the summit, the temperature plummeted, and they could feel deep rumblings within the rock, as if Pichincha had become aware of their presence. The Indian was beginning to grow nervous. They pulled themselves up and over a final ridge. Before them loomed the volcano's mouth, an awesome chasm with a circumference of at least a mile; it looked as if it could swallow the sun. The mountain trembled beneath their feet, and the crater belched smoke and sulfurous fumes.

They approached the brink of the abyss cautiously, almost on tiptoe, as if they were trying to sneak up on it without awakening the great beast that lay within. Suddenly Aldas cried out and sank chest deep into the snow. Pichincha had tricked them; unwittingly, Aldas had passed the actual brink. Now he was suspended from an extension made only of snow and ice. He could feel the heat from the fires below warming his feet.

The European lay down flat on the ice and grasped his guide's arms. He pulled, Aldas scrambled, and they made it back onto solid ground. The Indian was shaken, but his partner was undaunted. Now the European took the lead as they inched toward the rim of the crater. The steam from Pichincha's mouth had melted the snow off a rocky crag that jutted out from the rim. They crept gingerly out onto this long, narrow balcony over the volcano's maw. Sulfurous vapors choked them and violent tremors constantly shook their perch. Looking down, they beheld the abyss. In the depths, blue fires flickered. For Aldas, it seemed a view into the underworld itself. But for the European, it was a privileged look into the very heart of the earth, a chance to examine the forces that shaped and reshaped the face of the planet. Aldas looked at his companion to see his reaction to the fearsome view. The European was sprawled flat on his belly, gazing with contentment into the boiling darkness.

A Humboldt's-eye view of the terrain surrounding Ecuador's Pichincha volcano, which towers 15,173 feet above the rain forest. The explorer made thousands of sketches during his South American expeditions. This one was made shortly after he climbed to the top of Pichincha on May 26, 1802.

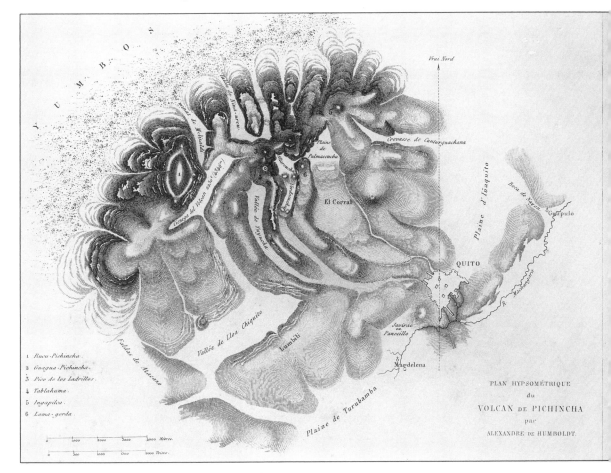

The young Alexander von Humboldt. Humboldt's fascination with the natural world began when he was a boy growing up on a Prussian estate. He spent hours hiking about the acres of land his family owned, collecting plants, flowers, insects, and rock specimens, which he would bring back to his room to study.

The man who gazed into live volcanoes was born Friedrich Wilhelm Karl Heinrich Alexander von Humboldt on September 14, 1769, in Berlin, the capital of Prussia. His father, Alexander Georg, baron von Humboldt, was a career soldier and court official. In his mid-forties, the baron retired to a life of leisure, devoting himself to duck hunting and entertaining at Schloss Tegel, the family estate located 12 miles north of Berlin. Alexander and his father occasionally roamed Tegel's woods together. These were wondrous journeys for the little boy, who was weak and often sick and spent much of his time confined to the house. The baron died when Alexander was only 10, but the legacy that he left to his son—a deep-seated love of nature—would prove to be the dominant force in Alexander's life, eventually leading him far from the gentle Brandenburg countryside. The boy's mother, the former Maria Elizabeth von Hollwege, bestowed an inheritance of a more material kind on her son: A wealthy woman in her own right, the owner of two estates and a town house in Berlin, she provided her son upon her death with the fortune that he would use to finance his South American odyssey.

No one who knew Humboldt when he was a boy ever imagined that he would develop into the robust, indefatigable world traveler he eventually became. He was an undersized and sickly child who rarely ventured out of the sight of his parents. Nor was there any evidence of the brilliant, tireless intellect that would one day make him the toast of his age. He was an easily distracted child, slow to learn, and because of his precarious health he could not go to school. Instead, tutors educated him at home. He received what was then considered to be a solid education, with training in the classics—the language, literature, and history of ancient Greece and Rome—history, modern languages, and mathematics. His tutors also taught him something of politics and economics because his mother hoped he would grow up to pursue a career in government. He was also exposed to botany and natural history.

Botany and natural history: These subjects alone truly captured the quiet boy's imagination. Whenever his parents allowed, he would escape to Schloss Tegel's wooded hills and the lake with its sandy beaches and nests of waterfowl. Picking up bugs, rocks, plants, flowers, and birds' eggs as he hiked, he would return home to sketch and label his specimens. His older brother, Wilhelm, began to call him the "little apothecary." When his parents did not allow him to go out, he spent his free time poring over maps and losing himself in travel tales. Later, remembering these early years, he wrote, "From my earliest youth I had felt an ardent desire to travel into distant regions, which Europeans had seldom visited. This desire is the characteristic of a period of our existence, when life appears an unlimited horizon."

As he got older, Humboldt began to shed the physical and mental lassitude of his childhood. His mind blossomed like one of the many splendid tropical flowers he would discover in the South American rain forests. His interests grew and became so wide ranging that they soon encompassed the entire spectrum of the natural and physical sciences. Truly a child of the Age of Reason, he studied and mastered the principles of botany, astronomy, electricity, physics, anthropology, chemistry, biology, anatomy, geology, and mineralogy. And he began to flower socially as well. Handsome, gregarious, and sharp witted, a brilliant conversationalist and an avid writer of letters, he formed friendships with people who shared his interests, such as Karl Ludwig Wildenow, a botanist, and Marcus Herz, a physician engaged in thrilling experiments with the newly discovered science of electricity.

Humboldt's mother, however, did not share his scientific inclinations, and she enrolled him in the University of Frankfurt an der Oder with the understanding that he would study economics. He spent the following year in Berlin learning the ins and outs of manufacturing, making new friends, and becoming something of a socialite. In the spring of 1789 he enrolled at the University of Göttingen, where he again studied economics. But he also found time to attend lectures in anatomy, anthropology, chemistry, physics, geology, and mineralogy. Here he also

Humboldt's father, Alexander Georg, baron von Humboldt, was an aristocrat and military officer. The baron encouraged young Alexander's curiosity about nature and often accompanied his son on his miniature expeditions around the grounds of the estate.

met Georg Forster, a naturalist who had accompanied the famed explorer Captain James Cook on his second Pacific voyage and who encouraged Humboldt to pursue his own dreams of scientific exploration. Such encouragement thrilled Humboldt, but how could he pursue his own dreams and fulfill the expectations of his mother as well?

Humboldt found a way. In 1791 he enrolled in the Freiberg College of Mining. At the Freiberg College he could study geology and geography and at the same time prepare for a career in the Prussian government's mining department. In Freiberg, Humboldt received practical training in geology and mineralogy, working in actual mines every morning. Lectures in geology, physics, chemistry, surveying, and law filled his afternoons. His nights were devoted to his own scientific pursuits, which included studying underground plant life and fossils. He developed keen powers of observation and strong laboratory techniques.

When Humboldt graduated from the mining school in 1792, the Prussian Bureau of Mines offered him an administrative position in Berlin, assuming that like most aristocrats he would want to stay in the city to take advantage of its cultural and social life. But Humboldt, to the astonishment of his superiors, asked to be sent to wild southern Prussia, an area rich in minerals. It did not take him long to make a name for himself there. Within a year he had increased sixfold the production of gold from mines others had thought were played out. But when his supervisor offered him a promotion in 1794—it would have been his second—Humboldt turned it down, informing him that he found the prospect of a career in mining less than satisfying.

Alexander's mother, the former Maria Elizabeth von Hollwege, came from a moneyed Berlin family and was independently wealthy. When she died in 1796, she left Alexander with a substantial inheritance; he wasted no time in using some of the money to finance a scientific expedition to South America.

In November 1796, Humboldt's mother died, leaving him a fortune so sizable that he no longer needed another income. He immediately resigned his position with the Bureau of Mines, ready at last to devote himself completely to his real goal—launching a scientific expedition far afield. Humboldt's initial attempts to organize and undertake an expedition were hampered by political tensions; the Napoleonic Wars made travel very difficult, and several planned journeys had to be aborted. In 1799, Humboldt joined forces with Aimé Bonpland, a young French physician and botanist. The intrepid Frenchman would prove to be the perfect traveling companion and scientific colleague. Bonpland was intelligent, unflappable, easily amused and frequently amusing to others, in good shape physically, and naturally brave.

In March 1799 the two would-be explorers finally got the break they had been hoping for. It was an extraordinary stroke of good fortune, surpassing Humboldt's greatest expectations. King Charles IV of Spain agreed to authorize an expedition to Spain's Central and South American colonies, virtually unknown territories that had been closed to most visitors for 300 years. The king hoped that Humboldt, who had had such great success in coaxing gold from supposedly exhausted mines in Prussia, would be able to locate gold and diamond deposits in the Americas; he granted Humboldt and Bonpland his protection. They were to travel wherever they pleased in the Spanish colonies, which included Cuba, Mexico, Venezuela, Colombia, Ecuador, Peru, Chile, Argentina, and the Philippines. To European ears, these were the alluring and exotic names of mysterious new worlds.

Humboldt and Bonpland began preparing for the expedition. Supplies were assembled. They bought, rented, or borrowed all the scientific devices they could lay their hands on, an eccentric array of instruments that could measure, interpret, record, and preserve for later inspection the various conditions and elements of the natural

Schloss Tegel, the Humboldt family estate in Brandenburg, in the kingdom of Prussia. Humboldt left Europe for South America in June 1799; it would be more than five years before he set eyes on his home again.

universe—as 18th-century man knew it—from the earth to the sky. The list of instruments was eight pages long and included compasses, scales, telescopes, microscopes, sextants and quadrants for sighting astronomical bodies and fixing locations, hygrometers and barometers for measuring humidity and air pressure, audiometers for analyzing gases, and various thermometers and chronometers. Appropriate clothing, climbing gear, and camping equipment were assembled as well.

By the spring of 1799 they were ready. But where would they go first? The Crown, while approving Humboldt's expedition, was not acting as a financial sponsor. Because Humboldt was funding the trip himself, he could devise any itinerary he wished. Hearing that the *Pizarro*, a Spanish packet, lay in port at La Coruña, readying for a voyage to Havana, Humboldt decided that he and Bopland would board it and begin their journey in Cuba.

On June 5, 1799, the *Pizarro* sailed with Humboldt, Bonpland, and their many cases and crates of books, notebooks, and scientific instruments safely stowed aboard. Humboldt never stayed in the cabin for too long; he spent the greater part of the voyage on deck, already engaged in scientific pursuits. By day he measured the temperature

and chemical composition of the sea, dropping overboard a thermometer or a small container attached to a line. He put out nets to trap marine life, which he then hauled aboard and sketched. Bonpland and Humboldt marveled at the creatures they caught. But the entire universe was Humboldt's laboratory, and he often turned his attention from sea to sky. During the day he measured the altitude of the sun, and by night he stargazed, using his astronomical observations to fix the *Pizarro*'s exact position at sea; the ship's captain was amazed when Humboldt used his calculations to correct the nautical maps.

But the *Pizarro* was ill starred and never made it to Cuba. Typhoid broke out on board, and it was not long before the passengers witnessed a burial at sea. Unless they went ashore immediately, the crew and passengers were in grave danger of falling victim to the disease. The captain veered away from Cuba and sailed for the nearest port—Cumaná, Venezuela. The ship made landfall in early July. As they drew closer to land, the sight of the massive continent, rising steadily from the sea to obliterate the horizon, erased any regrets Humboldt and Bonpland might have harbored about not reaching Cuba. They began preparing to go ashore.

D. JOSEF ANTONIO CABALLERO CAMPO,

Y HERRERA, Caballero Pensionado de la Real y distinguida
Orden de Cárlos Tercero; del Consejo de Estado de S. M.
y Secretario del Despacho Universal de Gracia y Justicia
de España é Indias.

Por quanto el REY ha concedido licencia á Sr. Humboldt
Prusiano, y a su Secretario para pasar á America á continuar el
estudio de Minas, y perfeccionarse en el conocimiento de otros
descubrimientos.

Por tanto manda S. M. á los Jueces de Arribadas de Indias de qua-
lesquiera Puertos de España, y demas personas á quienes correspon-
da, no le pongan impedimento alguno, á fin de que pueda embarcar-
se para el referido destino en la ocasion que mas le acomode; y á es-
te efecto expido el presente Pasaporte firmado de mi mano. Dado en
Aranjuez á diez y ocho de Marzo de mil setecientos noventa
y nueve.

Josef Antº. Caballero

In a Divine Country

Humboldt and Bonpland were ecstatic. They had not dreamed that there could be a place such as this. The overabundance of exotic plant and animal life and the sights and sounds and smells had an almost hallucinatory effect on the two Europeans. Modern sociologists and psychologists have a term for the two travelers' somewhat comical reaction to their new environment—culture shock. But for Humboldt and Bonpland, it was as if they had stumbled upon Eden itself. "We are here in a divine country," Humboldt wrote in his first, rapturous letter home. "We run around like the demented; in the first three days we were quite unable to classify anything; we pick up one object and throw it away for the next. Bonpland keeps telling me that he will go mad if the wonders do not cease soon."

But the wonders did not cease—they multiplied. Overwhelmed by the richness and fecundity of this world, Humboldt and Bonpland stayed in the vicinity of Cumaná for several months, as if they were afraid that they themselves might be assimilated into this seemingly unchecked profusion of insects, vegetation, and wildlife. For here everything seemed to feed upon everything else, and as they listened to the local Indians' tales of jaguars, 20-foot anacondas, monstrous crocodiles, vampire bats, voracious piranhas, and cannibal tribes, the two Europeans realized that in South America, man too was part of the food chain.

Part of the passport issued to Humboldt and authorized by the king of Spain, which enabled the explorer to travel freely throughout the Spanish territories of South America. "Acquisition of knowledge" was cited on the document as Humboldt's reason for traveling.

But it was not long before curiosity overcame trepidation and they began making the first excursions—by mule—into the rain forest that engulfed the lands surrounding the nearby coastal mountains.

In the South American rain forest Humboldt and Bonpland found a green, shadowy world teeming with life forms that were completely alien to the awed visitors. They followed trails that twisted between giant trees, wound through bamboo thickets, and wandered past enormous ferns. Above, the canopy of vines and foliage grew so thick that it blocked out the sun. Brilliantly colored flowers stood out sharply against the deep green jungle walls. Fantastic creatures observed the approach of the two explorers. Sloths, hanging upside down from branches, blinked at them with sluggish amazement. Kinkajous stared with huge, lustrous eyes. Powerful, lovely jaguars, almost invisible, slunk in the shadows, waiting for nightfall, while herds of peccaries (large, boarlike mammals) blundered noisily through the brush. There was a ceaseless insect racket, while strange monkeys and exotic birds shrieked and squawked at them from the trees, as if they were intent on alerting the entire rain forest to the arrival of the strangers.

Climbing into the mountains, the two visitors forded rushing, icy streams and skirted ravines that gaped like massive, open wounds. The paths they followed often narrowed to little more than 12 inches and passed behind breathtaking waterfalls that plummeted to unseen streams below. There were humans here as well. At a monastery nestled deep in a wild mountain valley, Humboldt and Bonpland were entertained by hospitable, self-sufficient Capuchin missionaries. The friars brought their guests to an enormous cave with an entrance 70 feet high—the Cavern of the Guacharo. Penetrating deep into the mountainside, it served as a home to thousands of *guacharos*, a species of odd-looking bird as yet unknown to Europeans.

Exhilarated, Humboldt and Bonpland returned to Cumaná and began packing their supplies; they sailed for Caracas, the capital of Venezuela, in November. They planned to wait out the rainy season there, after which they hoped to start on an extended journey into the Venezuelan interior. Located 160 miles west of Cumaná, Caracas was an enjoyable place. At 3,200 feet above sea level, it was blessed with cool breezes and a temperate climate. Humboldt and Bonpland rented an elegant house and spent the wet months resting and organizing the reams of data and the botanical specimens they had acquired. Hum-

To Humboldt and Aimé Bonpland, the Venezuelan rain forest seemed like a paradise, but they soon learned that they would need the assistance of the local Indians as guides and advisers if they hoped to survive passage through the interior.

Present-day Caracas, the capital of Venezuela. Humboldt and Bonpland spent the rainy season of 1799–1800 here. Ensconced in a stately old house, they wrote letters, cataloged the specimens they had collected, and planned their expedition into the rain forests of the interior.

boldt also questioned local Indians and missionaries about the Casiquiare, a natural canal—the only one of its kind in the world—that allegedly connected the Amazon and Orinoco river basins deep in southern Venezuela. Charles-Marie de La Condamine, a French scientist, had explored the Amazon River basin in 1744; he returned home to Europe the following year having heard tales of the Casiquiare, but he had failed to verify its connection with the Orinoco. Humboldt hoped to find and map the Casiquiare—if it actually existed.

On February 7, 1800, Humboldt and Bonpland left Caracas and plunged into the Venezuelan interior. They went west, crossing the coastal mountain range—the cordillera—and passing through forests of coffee trees and giant fig trees, occasionally stopping so Humboldt could examine the extensive veins of garnet crystals that permeated the mountain rock. At Lake Valencia, they drank the "milk," or creamy sap, of the *palo de vaca*, the cow tree. They came down out of the mountains in March. Now they were confronted with a new geographic challenge. Before them lay the llanos, the vast, grassy river plains that stretch across northern South America, covering an area roughly the size of Texas. The passage across the llanos would prove to be the first severe test of the travelers' endurance and stamina, for it was an inhospitable land, brutally hot and dusty. At times the temperature rose above 120 degrees, and mirages shimmered on the plains. In this unforgiving region they saw many crocodiles, snakes, and giant herds of cattle, but few men. The occasional water holes they came upon were always jealously guarded by the crocodiles.

Humboldt and Bonpland were understandably pleased to encounter fellow humans in this wasteland, at the ranching station of Calabozo. Here they were introduced to yet another biological marvel—the electric eel, a creature from 3 to 9 feet long that could incapacitate or kill large animals by administering electric shocks of up to 600 volts. Humboldt badly wanted to catch and dissect one of the eels, but this seemed impossible unless he was willing to absorb a substantial jolt. But the local Indians had a way: They drove horses and mules into a marshy pool, where they were repeatedly stung by the resident eels. Like living batteries, the eels eventually exhausted their electrical energy, whereupon they could be captured and handled safely. During his examination of the eels, Humboldt was stung nevertheless. "I do not remember," he wrote, "having ever received from the discharge of a large Leyden jar [an electrical apparatus] a more dreadful shock than the one I experienced when I very stupidly placed both my feet on an electric eel that had just been taken out of the water. I was affected for the rest of the day with a violent pain in the knees and almost every joint."

On March 27, 1800, having traveled roughly 108 miles, Humboldt and Bonpland reached the end of the llanos and straggled gratefully into the small town of San Fernando, which squats on the banks of the Apure River, one of the largest of the Orinoco's many tributaries. Eighty miles east of San Fernando, about midway in the Orinoco's journey to the Atlantic, the Apure flows into the Orinoco. The Orinoco itself is 1,600 miles long and forms a giant arc across Venezuela. From San Fernando, Humboldt's plan was to travel eastward down the Apure to the Orinoco and then southward up the Orinoco to another series of tributaries. From there he hoped to portage (travel overland) out of the Orinoco River basin to the Pimichin River, which is part of the Amazon River basin, and to follow the Pimichin to the Negro. The Negro, according to local Indians, would lead to the Casiquiare. Indians had traveled these rivers for millennia, and Spanish priests had built missions along them centuries before, but Humboldt would be the first scientist to explore the Orinoco River basin and, with luck, to find the Casiquiare.

Before daylight on March 30, Humboldt, Bonpland, and Nicholas Sotto, a Spaniard they met in San Fernando and invited to join them, loaded their supplies onto a large *lancha*, a dugout canoe with a palm-thatched cabin in the stern. The lancha was large enough to seat Humboldt, Bonpland, Sotto, an Indian servant, an Indian pilot, and four Indian rowers. Scientific instruments, plant presses, books, guns, and other provisions (their foodstuffs included live chickens, eggs, plantains, cassava, cocoa, brandy, sherry, oranges, and tamarinds) were stowed. The Europeans—in true European style—sat in chairs at a table under the shade of the palm roof while the Indians labored at the oars.

The party spent six days on the Apure. As the Indians rowed steadily, Humboldt devoted himself to scientific observations, analyzing river water, noting the river's features, and determining the latitude and longitude of major landmarks. Even in this, the dry season, the Apure was two miles wide. On April 5 they reached the junction with the Orinoco and began their journey up that river, which was even wider than the Apure. The Europeans were continually amazed at the abundance and variety of wildlife along the rivers. One day they came upon a small island that bristled colorfully with thousands of flamingos, pink spoonbills, and herons. Crocodiles 20 feet long dozed on the sandbanks, while rude groups of 50 or 60 capybaras— the capybara is the world's largest rodent, about the size of a full-grown hog—swam alongside the boat, threatening

The Humboldt expedition left Caracas and crossed the coastal cordillera in February and March 1800. Traveling by mule, they were frequently forced to dismount in order to lead the animals over particularly hazardous mountain trails.

to capsize it and plunge them all into the river. Humboldt also sighted tapirs (relatives of the rhinoceros), innumerable birds and monkeys, and more peccaries, piranhas, and stingrays. Some animals he never saw but only heard at night. Jaguars often approached the camp in the dark. (One evening, Humboldt, out in the jungle surrounding the camp, came withing 80 paces of a jaguar. Fortunately, the big cat did not notice him; Humboldt circled around the powerful animal and made it back to camp safely.) Bonpland, for his part, paid more attention to flora than to fauna, frequently going ashore to collect plant specimens from the grassland or rain forest that hugged the rivers. In the evenings he carefully pressed and classified his day's find.

At night the explorers would sometimes put ashore at a mission or plantation, if one was available. More often, however, they made camp alongside the water, sleeping in hammocks that were slung from trees or tied to canoe paddles stuck into the sandbanks. Humboldt described one of these camps in some detail: Edible provisions, he said, were protected above all else, forming the hub of a series of circles. Instruments and the animals and plants he and Bonpland were collecting would form the next circle. Then came Humboldt's, Bonpland's, and Sotto's hammocks, surrounded by those of the Indians. Finally, a circle of fires surrounded the entire party; they were kept burning all night to scare away jaguars. While the fires did help to keep away most of the big cats, they attracted crocodiles, who would sit and stare at them for hours. On a number of nights Humboldt or Bonpland had the unpleasant experience of awakening to find their circular campsite ringed in turn by the massive reptiles, their eyes shining balefully in the firelight.

Traveling up the lower Orinoco proved to be more difficult than traveling on the Apure; the Indians had to row against a strong current into heavy waves produced by high winds. In places the river was five miles wide, with sandy beaches and rocky mountains along its shores. Soon the voyage turned from difficult to unpleasant in the extreme. Clouds of gnats and mosquitoes tormented the party, and the stench of dead, rotting caimans (smaller, alligatorlike lizards) filled the air. These carcasses left the river's waters undrinkable, and Humboldt and his companions frequently went thirsty.

They stopped at an island where 300 Indians were encamped, each painted in their tribe's particular style. A month earlier, Humboldt learned, hundreds of thousands of turtles had laid eggs on this and other nearby islands. By now, he estimated, 30 million eggs lay under the sands. The Indians were waiting to harvest the eggs. Some they would dry; others they would make into oil; still others they would allow to hatch, for they considered baby turtles a delicacy.

Such turtle egg harvests attracted not only Indians but a few white missionaries as well, who came either to trade or proselytize. Coming upon another egg harvest on the island of Pararuma in April, Humboldt encountered a group of missionaries dressed in long blue robes, with shaved heads and long beards, seated on the ground playing cards and smoking pipes. The missionaries found Humboldt's party a bizarre sight. One of these holy fellows refused to accept Humboldt's explanation for his party's presence in such a godforsaken land. "How can anyone possibly believe," he demanded, "that you've left your own country to come here and be eaten by mosquitoes and measure lands that don't belong to you?" When the missionaries learned that Humboldt intended to press on to the upper Orinoco, through the terrible rapids of the Great Cataracts and to the lands beyond, they were astonished, and many of them made the sign of the cross. No one traveled beyond the Great Cataracts, they said, for those lands were filled with monsters and inhabited by peoples with only "one eye in the forehead" or with the "head of a dog" or a "mouth below the stomach."

The Europeans encountered many dangerous animals during their journey, but the one they feared most was the jaguar, a nocturnal predator that prowled around the perimeter of their campsites after dark. Fires were kept burning throughout the night to keep the big cats at bay.

To the Casiquiare

Despite the tales of monsters and cyclopes told by some of the priests at Pararuma, preparations to continue the expedition were made. The party took on some new members. One of the missionaries they encountered on the island, Father Bernardo Zea, claimed to know the way to the Casiquiare and agreed to guide them there and back. The original crew of Indians departed, and a new crew, consisting of local Indians who knew the rapids that lay ahead, "joined" the expedition (at least two went against their will; Zea locked them up the night before the departure in order to prevent their escape). Humboldt also bought the narrower canoe they would need to shoot the rapids. Far less comfortable than the first canoe, it was 40 feet long but only 3 feet wide. Four rowers sat in the bow while the pilot stood in the stern, just beyond another thatched hut built for the Europeans. (Humboldt soon grew disgusted with the hut, which was stifling during the day and trapped mosquitoes at night.) To add to the Europeans' discomfort, this canoe capsized so easily that they sometimes had to lie still in the bottom for hours while the Indians negotiated particularly dangerous waters.

By April 15 the rather crowded canoe had reached the end of the lower Orinoco. Putting ashore for the night, the party hiked a league inland along the narrow path that led from the river to Atures, one of Father Zea's missions. Humboldt delighted in the natural beauty of the mission's setting, in a savanna littered with huge granite boulders.

Humboldt (standing) and Bonpland (seated next to Humboldt), at a campsite deep within the rain forest, watch as Indians drag their canoe ashore while others prepare dinner. The Indians, who acted as guides, cooks, porters, navigators, and oarsmen, among other things, were indispensable to the European explorers.

At Atures, a mission on the lower Orinoco run by Father Zea, Humboldt and Bonpland were so tormented by a cloud of vicious, low-flying insects that they were forced to take refuge in a tree.

Exotic orchids stood out against the green fields. But Humboldt's delight faded as their visit lengthened. It was oppressively hot, and mosquitoes and small, venomous flies tormented them. At night, the hated *zancudos*—gnats noted for the painful, burning welts they raise with their long, sharp stingers—hovered constantly. The zancudos often made mission residents not only uncomfortable but sick; for eight months Zea had suffered from malaria. To escape the villainous little flies he had built himself a platform high in the trees. Only here could Humboldt and Bonpland quit slapping at insects long enough to dry their plants and make journal entries.

While Humboldt and Bonpland attempted to rest at the mission, eight Indians used ropes to haul the canoe through rapids so wild that Humboldt could hear their roar miles inland at Atures. On April 16 the rest of the party hiked to rejoin the canoe above the rapids. Back on the river, heavy rains made the going extremely difficult— they would progress 30 yards only to be pushed back 40. Late one night they arrived at the port of Maipurés. They hiked two hours in a ceaseless rain to another of Zea's missions. As they marched, a drenched Humboldt listened with amusement as the pilot tried to discourage him from continuing the expedition. "The Indian," Humboldt wrote, "who expressed himself with some facility in the Spanish, did not fail to talk to us of snakes, water-serpents, and tigers [jaguars] by which we might be attacked."

Again at the Maipurés rapids, the Indians pulled the canoe through while the Europeans waited at another mission, a neat and orderly community surrounded by groves of cassava and plantain trees—and blessedly free of insects. Climbing nearby Manimi Mountain, Humboldt and Bonpland had a bird's-eye view of the rapids, a sheet of white foam crashing around giant black rocks. On April 21 the canoe, only a little the worse for wear, came through the rapids, and Humboldt's party was river borne once more. Late at night on April 24 they left the Orinoco and

headed south, first on the Guaviare and then on the Atabapo River. The Atabapo was a friendly river that passed
through a region of almost supernatural beauty. Although
they were always damp from a constant rain, Humboldt
and his companions greatly enjoyed their time on the
Atabapo, a "black water" river. Its water, although almost
the color of coffee, was clean, cool, and delicious. Dense
green jungle lined the banks, channeling breezes down
the river and keeping the insects away. Cruising easily in
the steady rain or passing through the fine mists that hung
on the water, the travelers felt comfortable for the first
time in weeks. Fifteen-foot anacondas provided an escort,
swimming gracefully by the canoe's side for miles.

Refreshed, they reached the serpentine Temi River on
April 30. Instead of following the Temi's many twists and
turns, the Indians made good time by rowing the canoe
through the straighter, temporary channels formed by the
flooding that had resulted from the recent rains. Interfering
branches and vines were hacked away with machetes. The
rain forest itself was inundated, and the explorers found
themselves literally paddling through the treetops. Deep
in the quiet, shadowy depths of this aquatic forest, they
were astonished to find their canoe surrounded by a playful
school of dolphins—freshwater dolphins, thriving more
than 1,000 miles from the ocean.

On May 1 they arrived at the junction of the Temi and
the Tuamini. They advanced up the Tuamini and docked
at Javita, a mission community run by a Father Ceresco.
There, Humboldt hired 23 Indians to drag the canoe overland from the Tuamini to the Pimichin River, a tributary
of the Negro and part of the Amazon River basin. Although it was only nine miles from the Tuamini to the
Pimichin, it took four arduous days for the Indians to
transport the canoe. Because the ground was so soggy from
all the rain, the Indians had to create a makeshift road
out of branches cut from the surrounding forest. It took
the relatively unencumbered Humboldt, Bonpland, Sotto,

and Zea just a few hours to make the same journey. During the hike, Bonpland spent much of the time looking mournfully up into the rain forest canopy, where he could see a heaven of unknown, exotic plants and flowers. Unfortunately for the botanist, there was no way for him to get to them, for the canopy was at least 100 feet from the rain forest floor.

Arriving at a plantation of cacao trees near the Pimichin during the evening of May 5, the travelers spent the night in an abandoned hut. They all slept well, but in the morning a venomous snake was discovered under one of the jaguar skins they slept on. They were somewhat unnerved by the presence of their poisonous bedfellow and the thought that it had spent the night with them, for only the day before one of the Indians dragging the canoe had been bitten by a similar snake and had immediately lapsed into violent convulsions.

Arriving at the Pimichin, Humboldt was pleased to find the canoe still sound. Now, in a single day, it carried them down the Guinia River to the upper reaches of the Negro, one of the most lovely of the Amazon's multitude of tributaries. On the Negro they canoed for another day to San Carlos, a small Venezuelan fort on the border of Venezuela and Brazil, and the southernmost point they would attain on this expedition. Here, Humboldt briefly toyed with the idea of abandoning the search for the Casiquiare and instead taking the Negro to the Amazon, then following the Amazon all the way to its mouth on the Brazilian coast. The pull of the legendary, fearsome Amazon was strong, but Humboldt decided to stick with his original plan, for now, according to the Indians and Zea, they were within striking distance of the Casiquiare.

On May 10, 1800, just before sunrise, the party left San Carlos and sailed up the Negro. Just 10 miles north of San Carlos, the river bifurcated, the main stream flowing west while a massive offshoot—the Casiquiare—flowed east for 200 miles toward its eventual union with the Orinoco. The Casiquiare was a welcome and magnificent sight; Humboldt called it "as broad as the Rhine." The explorers rejoiced; they had achieved their goal. They went ashore, and Humboldt prepared to make the astronomical sightings and computations—using a sextant and a theodolite—necessary to determine the exact location of the entrance to the Casiquiare. He was worried that overcast skies might make this difficult, but on the night of May 11 he easily sighted the Southern Cross constellation and "the two beautiful stars which shine in the feet of the Centaur [the Centaurus constellation]." For Humboldt, this was perhaps the most rewarding moment of the trip, an intimate convergence of seemingly disparate elements of the natural universe—river and stars, with man acting as medium—that added yet another fragment of information to man's knowledge of his environment.

Now the return journey began; they would follow the Casiquiare back to the Orinoco. Humboldt later described these days as "the most painful part of our travels in [South] America." The Indians paddled for up to 14 hours a day

When they were not hiking overland, the members of the Humboldt expedition traveled on the South American rivers in lanchas, *large dugout canoes with thatched cabins of palm leaves and bamboo. The Indians, using poles and oars, provided the manpower to propel the* lancha *when the current ran against it.*

against fast currents, through turbulent rapids and between toppled trees. The weather made everybody miserable—no breeze relieved them and the temperature hovered near 90 degrees night and day. The high humidity made the party even more uncomfortable, and it also ruined many of the plant specimens Bonpland had worked so hard to collect and preserve—a bitter blow to the Frenchman. Insects fed on the travelers, and their faces and hands became swollen and bloody. Low on provisions, they became so hungry and thirsty that they ate plain, bitter powdered chocolate and drank great quantities of muddy river water, which sickened them. Two days into this leg of the journey, they entered territory so wild that Humboldt half expected to see some of the strange sights the missionaries had warned of back at Pararuma. Often they had to hack

Humboldt's sketch of a cacajao monkey. The explorers encountered a wide variety of monkeys, including night monkeys, titis, sakis, howler monkeys, capuchin monkeys, squirrel monkeys, spider monkeys, woolly monkeys, and marmosets.

a space out of the jungle in order to land for the night. The jaguars here were huge and bold; one night they came close enough to camp to carry off the expedition's dog.

Nevertheless, Humboldt remained irrepressibly cheerful and continually fascinated by his surroundings. Bonpland took pleasure in his plant collecting, and both enjoyed the menagerie they had been assembling throughout the trip. In fact, by now the canoe resembled a floating zoo. At a mission on the canal Humboldt bought a young toucan and a magnificent purple macaw. He especially liked watching the antics of the toucan as it bathed, fished, and teased the many little monkeys on board, whom Humboldt described as "sad and passionate." Father Zea complained about the animals—the canoe now housed 11 birds and 8 monkeys; some were kept in willow cages, but some had free run of the canoe—but he allowed the tiny, timid titi monkeys to hide in the sleeves of his habit whenever it rained. Humboldt also passed a memorable day on

Despite the rigors of their journey, Humboldt (seated) and Bonpland were anything but light travelers; wherever they went, scientific books and instruments as well as a vast array of flora and fauna—both living and dead—went with them. (Note the monkey sleeping happily on the floor.)

the Casiquiare listening to one of his Indian rowers describe his eating preferences, which included human
palms.

They reached the Orinoco on May 21. Twenty miles
upstream they stopped for the night at Esmerelda, a tiny
mission. Situated on a wide plain at the foot of the Sierra
Duida, Esmerelda proved ideally suited for its function as
a purgatorial place of exile for recalcitrant missionaries.
Often clouds of insects became so thick that they blotted
out the sun. And during the dry season, so little grew in
the area that residents resorted to eating ground fishbones.
But Humboldt found even Esmerelda fascinating; for him,
the high point of their stay came when an Indian showed
him how to make curare, a poison used by the local Indians
to paralyze humans or animals. Humboldt even swallowed
some of the poison in his attempt to learn more about it.

Informed that fierce Guiaco and Guaharibo Indians
would surely attack—and eat—the party if they continued

*Humboldt (seated), Bonpland,
and an Indian observe a meteor
shower from the terrace of a house
on the South American coast.
Humboldt was a dedicated
astronomer, and he often turned
his attention from the earth to
the heavens.*

on up the Orinoco, they instead returned downstream. On a wide, calm section of river bordered by jungle, the Indian rowers enjoyed a respite. Sometimes they let the canoe drift on the current all night long. Traveling swiftly now, the Humboldt party reached the Atures rapids once more on May 31. Here, Father Zea took leave of the expedition. Next, Humboldt made a detour for a short grave-robbing excursion to the cavern of Ataruipe, which Zea had told him about. The burial ground of the extinct Atures Indians, Ataruipe turned out to be a dank cave filled with mummified skeletons; some had been bleached white and others painted red. Stealing several skulls and three skeletons, Humboldt quickly wrapped them and smuggled them back to the canoe. Despite his assertions that he carried only crocodile and manatee bones, the Indians recognized his cargo by the smell of the resin used to preserve the skeletons; Humboldt had trouble persuading any Indians to join his crew for the rest of his journey, for none of them wanted to travel with the dead.

On June 5 the party reached the village of Uruana, where Humboldt made notes on the local Indians' use of hallucinogenic plants and their habit of eating dirt. Four days and 100 miles later, Sotto disembarked. Once again coming to the confluence of the Apure and the Orinoco, Humboldt and Bonpland did not reenter the Apure but continued east along the Orinoco to Angostura, a town located only 150 miles from the Venezuelan coast. They had covered more than 1,500 miles, and their journey was almost at an end. Only the llanos lay between them and the coast. This was fortunate; the expedition had taken its toll. The two Europeans were weak and emaciated, and both were suffering from typhoid fever. Humboldt recovered fairly quickly, treating himself with a local remedy, but Bonpland almost died. It took a month for the Frenchman to regain enough strength to cross the llanos. They arrived at their point of origin, Cumaná, in November, and both men rejoiced at the sight of the ocean.

The Quindío Pass

Humboldt's first South American journey—he would embark on another before too long—had a profound effect on the small body of European knowledge about that part of the world. After the expedition, the "lost world" of eastern South America was not quite so lost, and it never would be again. Thousands of previously unknown plant and animal specimens had been collected, obscure Indian tribes had been discovered, 1,500 miles of river and rain forest had been charted, and the longitude and latitude of 55 locations had been fixed. Myths had been exploded and new mysteries uncovered.

Humboldt's journey of discovery had a profound impact on him as well. Since his early days as a fledgling naturalist in Prussia, theories concerning the true nature of the universe had been germinating in his mind, and in the fecund atmosphere of South America's rain forests, these theories had begun to flower. Trudging through the lush and savage jungles, Humboldt saw evidence, day after day, that all nature was part of one great, single process. Indeed, it became apparent to him that all of the cosmos, from the damp earth underfoot to the brilliant, distant stars overhead, was interrelated, and that all its seemingly diverse elements actually interacted on a continual and intimate basis. That this dance of life did exist had been proved to Humboldt in the rain forests and on the rivers, on the mountains and in the skies of South America. But his appetite for knowledge had only been whetted—he wanted to probe deeper, to see behind the dance, to get a glimpse

Humboldt emerged from the South American interior in November 1800. Exhausted and feverish, he sailed to Havana, the capital of Cuba, for a rest. By spring 1801 he was refreshed and ready to return to South America in the hope this time of exploring the formidable Andes Mountains.

of the fundamental patterns and laws that governed the dance. Alexander von Humboldt was searching for nothing less than evidence of God in nature.

For the immediate future, however, what Humboldt and Bonpland needed most was rest. They decided to spend the winter on the island of Cuba, hoping to find some of the comforts and trappings of European city life in Havana, Cuba's capital. They sailed from Venezuela on November 24, 1800. Their voyage was less than pleasant, however; misadventure seemed to dog their footsteps. The passage to Cuba was alternately stalled by calms and beset by storms, and the small wooden vessel caught fire only a week out into the Caribbean Sea—the crew managed to douse the flames and they sailed on. After 25 days at sea they docked in Havana. Once they had a chance to mend, Humboldt intended to board another ship and sail to North America, where they might undertake a tour of Canada and the Great Lakes and then embark on a cruise down the Ohio and Mississippi rivers to New Orleans. From there, Humboldt suggested, they could head for Mexico, the Philippines, and the East Indies. If all went as planned, by the time they made landfall in Europe once again they would have circumnavigated the globe.

By now, however, Humboldt and Bonpland knew that things rarely went as planned, and in early 1801 they learned from an American newspaper report that the French scientific expedition led by Captain Baudin—an expedition Humboldt and Bonpland had been invited to join back in 1799—had finally set sail and would make Peru within the year. Humboldt once again changed his plans. He was eager to link up with the Baudin party; instead of going to North America, he and Bonpland would make for the Peruvian coast in an attempt to join Baudin in Lima. (Unlike some scientists and explorers, who somewhat jealously liked to keep their own discoveries and data separate from the findings of their peers, Humboldt was always eager to share his own work with others, in the hope that synthesis would yield new knowledge.) It seemed that Alexander von Humboldt was destined to return to South America.

But first there were matters at hand to attend to. Most importantly, arrangements had to be made for the shipment to Europe of the plant, mineral, and animal specimens the explorers had collected in Venezuela as well as the volumes of charts, sketches, and other written data they had compiled. This was a rather unnerving prospect for Humboldt and the Frenchman—they already knew too well the erratic nature of mail service across the Atlantic. So far, Humboldt had received but three of the many letters his brother, Wilhelm, a faithful correspondent, had sent to the New World. In writing home to family and friends, Humboldt took to repeating news, knowing his previous letters most likely had not arrived. Committing the precious yield of their Venezuelan expedition to such a perilous journey troubled Humboldt and Bonpland deeply. "Nothing makes me more anxious than the safety of manuscripts and herbariums," Humboldt confessed.

Humboldt and Bonpland carefully split up their notes and specimens, retaining some for their own use but sending one herbarium to France and another to England via the United States. They also sent to Bonpland's brother by a third ship a manuscript describing new and rare plant species. And indeed they did well to split up their treasures so—arriving home three years later they would find that one of the ships had sunk, while the British had captured another. (The specimens captured by the British eventually fell into the hands of Sir Joseph Banks, the noted British naturalist who had accompanied Captain Cook on his first voyage.)

Humboldt also spent a good part of his three months in Cuba touring the island and taking notes for a geography he planned to write. In Havana, a walled city that almost equaled the size of New York, and where "one walked through ankle-deep mud and suffered the stench of salted meat," he brought out his surveying instruments to make an exact measurement of the port's latitude and longitude (mapmakers of the day often lacked accurate information about the location of even such important cities; Humboldt was the cartographer's best friend). In Cuba's interior he visited plantations and factories, observing the cultivation and processing of sugar, indigo, tobacco, and cotton. In his geography A *Political Essay on the Island of Cuba*, Humboldt would record his abhorrence of the slavery that so enriched the island's economy. And believing that "it is for the traveller who has been an eyewitness to the suffering and degradation of human nature to make the complaints for the benefit of the oppressed," he became an ardent abolitionist and worked for the rest of his life for the passage and enforcement of laws against the slave trade. Humboldt was as much a humanist as he was a scientist and naturalist.

Humboldt and Bonpland set sail from Cuba on March 8, 1801, beginning the journey that would ensure them a place in history and make the name *Humboldt* the toast of the civilized world. Their ultimate goal was Lima, Peru, but their initial destination was the magnificent walled city of Cartagena, a port on the northern Colombian coast. From Cartagena they planned to traverse the Isthmus of Panama so Humboldt could map a canal route. Once across the isthmus, Humboldt hoped to sail to Guayaquil, an Ecuadorian port on the western coast of South America, and from there they might move on to Lima. But once again a change of plans was called for. This time, nature itself seemed to be directing Humboldt's journey; the winds did not favor a passage from Panama to Guayaquil and could not be expected to until the season changed. Humboldt acquiesced to the will of the elements and decided to make a journey overland from Cartagena across the northwestern corner of South America to Peru. Thus he hoped not only to save time but to meet Father José Celestino Mutis, a renowned botanist who resided in Bogotá,

(continued on page 57)

Paradise Found

When Alexander von Humboldt and the botanist Aimé Bonpland arrived in South America in 1799, they were astounded by the profusion of exotic flora and fauna they encountered in the lush rain forests and verdant cordilleras of that continent. Humboldt described South America as "divine," and for the botanist and the naturalist it was indeed a paradise. During their five-year exploration of Venezuela, Colombia, Ecuador, and Peru, Humboldt and Bonpland cataloged and sketched hundreds of animals that were still unheard of in Europe; they also collected thousands of plant specimens, which they preserved and shipped back to the Old World. Upon returning from South America, Humboldt used what remained of his own personal fortune to commission talented artists, who embellished his sketches of animals and painted intricately detailed, true-to-life pictures of the plant specimens. The results of the artists' labors—including the pictures seen here—were subsequently displayed in Paris exhibitions and in the volumes Humboldt published, and they delighted and fascinated European audiences and readers.

Simia leonina (lion monkey)

Tab. 95.

Anguloa superba

Rhexia lepidota

Paspalum humboldianum

Dendrobium grandiflorum

Tab. 8.

Peperomia talinifolia

Pl. XXX.

Simia ursina (bear monkey)

Simia melanocephala (black-headed monkey)

Simia satanas (devil monkey)

Vultur gryphus (Andean condor)

(continued from page 48)

Colombia, and also to map some of the unknown South American territory north of the Amazon.

The elements continued to vex the explorers, however, and for a time Humboldt despaired of even reaching Colombia. Approaching Cartagena on March 30, 1801, their ship ran into a gale so strong that it almost capsized. In fact, all aboard were about to give themselves up for lost when a change in the sail suddenly righted the boat. They found safe haven in a cove, where they anchored to wait out the storm. During the night, Humboldt took a small boat ashore in order to get a clearer view of an eclipse, only to be set upon by a gang of escaped convicts. The peaceful explorer managed to escape, and he and Bon-

After a 500-mile journey up the Magdalena River, the Humboldt party arrived in the tiny Colombian town of Honda in June 1801. From there they began the ascent into the Andes.

pland were extremely grateful to arrive intact in Cartagena the next day.

Once they were safely within the walls of the historic Colombian city, Humboldt and Bonpland boxed up the heaviest of their instruments and sent them on ahead. From Cartagena they themselves hiked southeast 20 miles to Turbaco, where Humboldt delightedly explored the local gas volcanoes. From Turbaco they journeyed another 30 miles eastward across Colombia's coastal plain to its major river—the Magdalena. On April 21, with little fanfare, they started up the Magdalena in a canoe rowed by 20 Indians, and within a few days they found themselves once again swallowed up by the endless rain forests of South America.

The 500-mile journey up the Magdalena was as grueling as any of their previous river passages. The jungle they passed through was ancient and virtually impenetrable. Only occasionally did they see the smoke of Indian campfires, although crocodiles, parrots, and monkeys were their constant companions. After a month on the river, the Europeans began to feel that they had passed out of the 19th century and were rowing backward in time, into the

Leaving the tropical lowlands behind, the explorers journeyed to Colombia's capital, Bogotá, which is situated on a plateau in the eastern Andes, 8,563 feet above sea level. The travelers, especially Bonpland, who was suffering from malarial fevers, welcomed the cool mountain air.

prehistoric jungles of the planet's earlier days; they almost expected to see dinosaurs feeding on the abundant foliage. The Indians, in the meantime, battled a strong current fed by constant thunderstorms. Eight became so exhausted that Humboldt had to send them home. Others developed foul-smelling ulcers in the constant damp. Humboldt and Bonpland managed to maintain their health, however, and devoted themselves, respectively, to charting the course of the river and collecting plants and tropical fruits. In June they reached the tiny village of Honda, and their journey on the timeless Magdalena was over.

From Honda, according to their map, Humboldt and Bonpland had only to travel 50 miles eastward to Bogotá, capital of Colombia. This seemed like a laughable distance compared to the 500 miles they had just covered, but even this portion of their journey would prove arduous. Whereas Honda lies in the tropics on a flat river plain, Bogotá is situated 9,000 feet higher, on a plateau in the hulking Andes Mountains. Humboldt and Bonpland hired guides, purchased mules, carved two stout walking sticks for themselves, and set off for Bogotá. The road from Honda to Bogotá often amounted to little more than a path of steep steps leading ever upward. Sometimes no more than a foot and a half wide—hardly wider than the mules the party rode—this path climbed inexorably between natural rock walls and through an amazing array of plant life. Forests of nutmeg, walnut, and cinchona trees at the lower altitudes gave way to mountain laurels and conifers farther up. Humboldt was fascinated with the changes in vegetation that occurred with altitude, and he kept careful records as they climbed. Bonpland, however, was especially miserable on this leg of the journey; he suffered from fever, headaches, and nausea—symptoms of malaria. Not until they had reached the plateau that cradles Bogotá did the Frenchman feel the relief of a cool breeze.

On the plateau, Humboldt and Bonpland found that an Indian had run ahead to announce their arrival; a parade of finely dressed horsemen had galloped out past the fields and Indian villages surrounding Bogotá to greet the travelers. Humboldt and Bonpland were obliged to get off their mules, and they were driven into the city in fine European-built carriages. By the time they reached the city a crowd of citizens—including a drove of scampering children—had joined the procession. Those who had not joined the parade hung out of their windows, straining for a glimpse of the foreigners, two of the very few who would journey to Bogotá during the Spanish colonial era. Later that day the entire city honored Humboldt and Bonpland with a banquet.

Because of Bonpland's illness, he and Humboldt stayed in Bogotá for two months. Humboldt hardly regretted this delay—it gave him ample time to compare notes with the great botanist Father Mutis. Humboldt certainly found Mutis's reputation as the leading authority on South American flora well founded; since arriving in Colombia 40 years earlier the Spaniard—now 70 years old—had collected 20,000 plants. (A group of 30 artists had been commissioned by the king to draw thousands of these specimens). Humboldt made extensive use of Mutis's herbarium and his library of books on botany, a treasure trove of information. The old Spaniard, for his part, was as impressed with Humboldt as Humboldt was with him. Mutis did everything possible to make his guest comfortable. He even temporarily evicted his sister-in-law from a house he owned next door to his own so that Humboldt might stay as close as possible to him. Humboldt did not spend all his time indoors studying, however; he also made excursions into the surrounding countryside, to the nearby mountains that rose high above Bogotá's plateau, and to Lake Guatavita. On these jaunts he discovered not only rock salt and coalfields but fossilized mastodon bones.

Humboldt—proudly carrying 100 botanical paintings given to him as a gift by Mutis—and a rested Bonpland finally left Bogotá on September 8, 1801. Their destination was Quito, Ecuador, a city some 4 months and 500 miles to the southwest. To reach Quito, their party would travel farther into the Andes Mountains, that vast stretch of high plateaus and higher peaks that stands watch over the entire western South American coast. On the first leg of this journey, their pack train traveled west from Bogotá and back down into the Magdalena River valley, then up into the Andes on the other side of the valley. (The Colombian Andes east of the Magdalena are known as the Cordillera Oriental, or eastern range, and those west as the Cordillera Central, the central range.) Ahead lay territory so wild and inhospitable that they had to pack provisions for a month.

Now the explorers ascended into a different South America, a harrowing landscape of cloud-enshrouded peaks and timeless mountain valleys; of narrow paths winding above dizzying cliffs; of clear, icy mountain lakes; and of the ghostly, overgrown ruins of the ancient Inca Empire.

The volcanic desert surrounding the town of Pasto, which is situated atop a high Andean plateau, presented the Europeans with one of the most desolate landscapes they encountered during their travels throughout South America.

A harrowing 4-month traversal of the Andes brought Humboldt and Bonpland to Quito, Ecuador, a town perched at an altitude of 9,300 feet. Humboldt called Quito, which is surrounded by gigantic volcanoes, a town that slept "on the edge of catastrophe."

They climbed through bamboo thickets and lush forests of white-trunked wax palms. Underfoot grew beautiful ferns, passionflowers, fuchsias, and orchids. Beyond the city of Ibagué, located 80 miles west of Bogotá, they entered the treacherous Quindío Pass. At 12,000 feet above sea level, the pass led them through rock-walled ravines 20 feet deep. Trees grew so thick overhead that they could not see the sky. Meeting a pack train headed in the opposite direction, they had to scale the sides of the ravine, holding on to the roots of the trees above, in order to let the fellow travelers pass.

They came down out of the Quindío Pass, walking in a pouring rain and over sharp bamboo shoots that shredded their boots and left their feet bloody, to the town of Cartago. From Cartago they headed south for approximately 150 miles to the town of Popayán, located in the breathtaking Cauca Valley. Here they stayed for the month of November, collecting plants and climbing Puracé, a nearby volcano that towered 15,600 feet above sea level and loudly belched huge jets of steam. As the rainy season began, they climbed back into the Andes, heading for the city of Pasto, which lay another 100 miles to the southwest. This would be the hardest leg of their journey. In the torrential downpour, flash floods and mud slides were a constant threat; lightning danced around the mountain peaks, and thunder rolled through the valleys. Humboldt later recalled passing through "thick woods interspersed with swamps, where the mules sank up to their girths, and narrow paths winding through such rocky clefts that one could almost fancy one was entering a mine, and the road paved with bones of mules that had perished from cold or fatigue."

The cold, barren desert plateau surrounding Pasto presented an otherworldly appearance—the mountains of the moon would hardly have seemed more desolate. Sleet and snow, driven by high winds, raked the plateau, and low clouds mixed with volcanic fumes to form a drifting fog that alternately obscured and revealed strange vistas. Sometimes, finding no shelter on the high plains, they passed the cold and rainy nights in tents that their Indian guides made out of leaves. They celebrated Christmas in the small town of Pasto. On January 6, 1802, they reached Quito, the capital of Ecuador, a town cradled by massive, active volcanoes. They were given a grand reception in Quito—some of the oldest colonial families resided there—and there were dinners and affairs in their honor almost nightly. Bonpland greatly enjoyed the attention of Quito's noble families and especially the young ladies. Humboldt, however, only had eyes for the great volcanoes that rumbled and smoked ominously above the town. Quito, Humboldt wrote, was a town that slept "in peace on the edge of catastrophe."

A Dreadful Abyss

Humboldt had originally planned to spend no more than a few weeks in Quito, but he was forced to change his plans—yet again—when he learned that Baudin's French expedition would not, after all, land along the Peruvian coast, having actually taken an eastern route around Africa rather than a western route around South America. But by then, Humboldt wrote in a letter home, he and Bonpland had grown "accustomed to such disappointments," and they consoled themselves "in the thought that we had been prompted by a purpose in all the sacrifices we had made. In going over our herbariums, our barometric and trigonometric observations, our drawings, and our experiments on the atmosphere of the Cordilleras, we see no reason for regretting our visit to countries that have remained largely unexplored by scientists. We have come to feel that man ought not to count upon anything which he cannot obtain by his own enterprise." And indeed, the aborted rendezvous with the French party proved to be a propitious turn of events, for it allowed Humboldt to embark on what many—himself included—considered his greatest enterprise: the assault on Chimborazo, at the time the highest known peak in the world.

To each of the local volcanoes—Cotopaxi, Antisana, Tungurahua, Iliniza, Pichincha, and Chimborazo—Humboldt devoted two to three weeks of study and observation. He climbed each one in turn, examined their

The terrain around Quito inspired awe in the visitors, and each new day of exploration brought spectacular sights. Humboldt was irresistibly attracted to the area's most dangerous feature—the volcanoes.

geologic structure, analyzed the gas content of their ex-
halations, timed their seismic waves, and measured the
composition of the atmosphere surrounding them. Sometimes Bonpland or an Indian guide accompanied him on
his ascents. Others he made alone. Merely to climb these
peaks, all of which stand over 15,000 feet, represented a
formidable challenge. Today's mountaineers use sophis-
ticated equipment and techniques and wear clothing especially designed for their task. But in 1802 few significant
climbs had been attempted, so Humboldt could not draw
on others' experience but had to devise his own techniques
for climbing and acclimatization. (One of the main obstacles was altitude sickness, and Humboldt was well ac-
quainted with its symptoms by the time he challenged
Chimborazo.) Modern "free climbers"—purists who es-
chew the use of ropes and other mountaineering equipment—would have embraced Humboldt as one of their
own.

On June 9, 1802, Humboldt, Bonpland, a young Ec-
uadorean named Carlos Montúfar, the son of the local
governor, and several Indian guides set out east on a trip
of approximately 50 miles to Chimborazo. On June 23
they arrived at the base of the hulking volcano and began
their ascent. It was an arduous and harrowing experience
from the start, requiring, as Humboldt put it, "extreme
exertion and considerable patience," not to mention cour-
age. Soon they were literally climbing through the clouds,
breaching one cloud bank only to find themselves enveloped by another. Visibility within these areas was almost
nil; the climbers became mere shadows in the cottony mist.
At the snow line, all but one of the Indians deserted.
Humboldt found this rather amusing. "It is a peculiar
characteristic of all such climbing trips in the Andes," he
wrote, "that beyond the snow line Europeans are invari-
ably left without guides just at the point . . . where help
is most needed."

The higher the four men climbed, the more difficult—

and terrifying—the conditions became. "In many places," Humboldt wrote, "the ridge was not wider than eight to ten inches! To our left was a precipice of snow whose frozen crust glistened like glass. The angle of this icy slope was thirty degrees. On the right lay a fearful abyss, from 800 to 1,000 feet deep, huge masses of rocks projecting from it." The climbers were now using both hands and feet as they went, and the jagged rock bloodied their palms and fingers. "Painfully cut," they continued upward. Humboldt was also suffering from an infected insect bite on his foot, and it began to torment him.

In Humboldt's day, Chimborazo, at 20,561 feet the highest of the volcanoes around Quito, was generally accepted to be the tallest mountain in the world. After climbing the other volcanoes in the area, Humboldt set his sights on Chimborazo.

Unable to see the summit, the climbers halted on a tiny ridge to rest and calculate their altitude. Humboldt, using a tube barometer, discovered that they were at 17,300 feet. They continued the ascent, moving up the face of the

Humboldt's sketch of the volcanic Cordillera de Quito. Among the volcanoes that he climbed and charted during his stay at Quito were Cotopaxi, Antisana, Tungurahua, Iliniza, Pichincha, and Chimborazo.

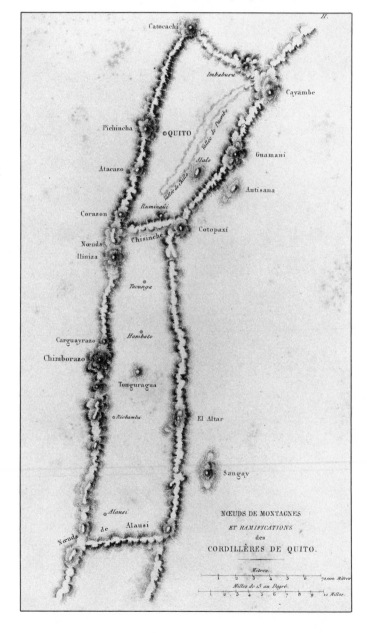

volcano like four insects, inch by inch. About an hour later they began to have trouble breathing, and the altitude sickness began: "One after another we all began to feel sick from nausea and giddiness. . . . Blood exuded from the lips and gums, and the eyes became bloodshot." Humboldt was unimpressed by these symptoms, having become familiar with them on his previous climbs. They pushed onward.

As they neared the peak of the volcano, "the stratum of mist which had hidden every distant object began to clear. Once more we recognized the dome-shaped summit of Chimborazo, now very close. What a grand and solemn spectacle! The very sight of it renewed our strength. The rocky ridge, which only had a thin sprinkling of snow here and there, became somewhat wider. With this surer surface underfoot we hurried on—only to be stopped dead in our tracks by a ravine some 400 feet deep and 60 feet wide. This was an insurmountable barrier. The softness of the snow and the steepness of the slopes made it impossible to scale the sides."

Again Humboldt consulted the barometer. They had attained an altitude of 19,286 feet—higher than any human had ever climbed. They could go no higher, however. Numbed by the cold, their hands bloody, their boots soaked through by the icy snow, they decided to stay no longer in "this dreary waste, for we were soon enveloped in mist again, which hung about us motionless. We saw no more of the summit of Chimborazo, nor of the neighboring Sierra Nevada, still less the high plain of Quito. We felt as isolated as in a balloon."

They began their retreat down the mountain, finding that "even greater caution was necessary than during the ascent." Despite their discomfort and the increasingly ominous weather, Humboldt stopped along the way to chip off some specimens of the volcanic rock. Then, having gotten all they could out of Chimborazo, they continued the descent. Chimborazo, however, was not quite finished with them; the volcano presented the trespassers with a few parting gifts: "When we were at a height of about 17,400 feet we ran into a violent hailstorm and twenty minutes later into a snowstorm so heavy that the ridge was soon several inches deep." Despite the volcano's treachery, the climbers made it down safely. They were frozen, bruised, and exhausted but also exultant in the knowledge that they had accomplished what no man had before. As the news of the heroic deed found its way out of the Andes and across the seas to Europe and North America, the fame of Humboldt spread and grew with it. By the time he emerged from South America in 1803, he had become a living legend.

Although he knew that he would not meet Baudin there, Humboldt decided to push on to Lima, Peru. Now accompanied by Carlos Montúfar as well as Bonpland, he traveled down out of the highlands and into a less harsh environment. As they headed toward Riobamba, a city about 200 miles due south of Quito, they encountered more Inca ruins, and Humboldt became fascinated with that lost civilization, which was at its peak from the mid-15th to the mid-16th centuries. At Riobamba, he spent most of his time talking with an Indian who was in possession of a priceless treasure—a 16th-century Indian manuscript that chronicled events before the Spanish conquest. Humboldt spent hours poring over the manuscript. This codex supported a theory that he had formulated during his South American travels—that the Indians of the New World had originated in Asia. As usual, his analysis was right on the money and well ahead of its time. His exposure to the relics of the rich Inca culture also increased his distaste for colonial rule in South America, and he correctly predicted a time when the people of that continent would throw off the imperialist yoke and form independent republics.

From Riobamba the party went on to the town of Cuenca. Here, Humboldt halted long enough to visit the ruins of a spectacular Inca palace cut from solid rock. From Cuenca, they headed due south for almost 200 miles, into the plains of the upper Amazon. Humboldt described this area as "an unknown world rich in magnificent vegetation." Even in this wilderness, Humboldt discovered, the Indians communicated easily with friends or relatives in the large cities on the coast; native couriers, with mail tucked inside their turbans, regularly drifted downstream on rivers heading toward the Pacific. Following an Inca highway back into the Andes and across the *páramos*—cold, windswept regions—toward Cajamarca,

Drawn by Humboldt, this diagram of Chimborazo charts the altitudinal distribution of plant life on the volcano; it is an example of the science of plant geography that he developed during his travels throughout South America.

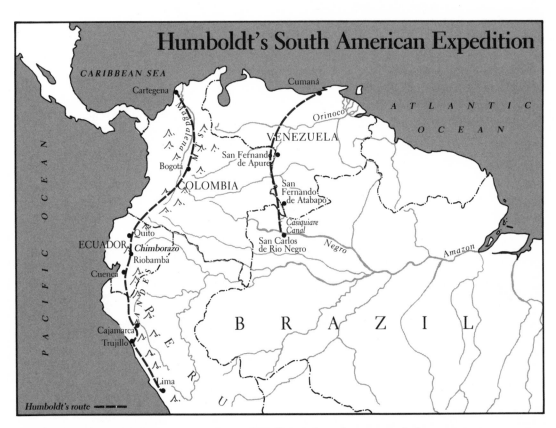

Humboldt's South American Expedition

The first leg of Humboldt's South American expedition took him from Cumaná, on the Venezuelan coast, to the Casiquiare, which links the Negro, a tributary of the Amazon, to the Orinoco. The second leg of the journey began at the coastal city of Cartagena, Colombia, followed the Magdalena River into the Colombian Andes, and took him steadily southward along the Andes and through Ecuador until he reached Lima, Peru.

an ancient Inca city, they crossed the magnetic equator. Humboldt's measurement of the magnetic intensity of the earth here would serve as a base measure against which all other geomagnetic readings would be compared for the next 50 years. At Cajamarca, Humboldt toured the ruins of the palace of Atahuallpa, an Inca prince, and he was shown the small room where the conquistadores had imprisoned Atahuallpa in 1532. From Cajamarca, they started out on the final leg of their odyssey. As they came down the western slope of the Andes to the Peruvian coast, Humboldt caught sight—for the first time—of the Pacific Ocean. "We saw it distinctly in the glitter of a vast light," he wrote, "an immeasurable expanse of ocean."

In October 1802, the expedition reached sea level at the city of Trujillo. From here they crossed the great Peruvian coastal plain, making Lima in late October. They spent two months in Lima, arranging and packing up the plant and rock specimens they had collected during the long journey from Cartagena. Humboldt turned his attention to the heavens once again, observing the transit of the planet Mercury across the sun. He then devoted himself to an endeavor of a more earthly nature, collecting samples of guano (bird droppings), an extremely effective fertilizer that the Inca had taken advantage of. Humboldt sent the precious guano, among other things, home to Europe.

Humboldt, Bonpland, and Carlos Montúfar sailed from Callao, Peru, a port on the Pacific coast, on Christmas Eve, 1802. Their destination was Guayaquil, Ecuador. On board the *Causino*, the tireless Humboldt broke out his gadgets and went to work. He devoted the entire voyage to a study of the cold current that runs along the western coast of Peru, now known as the Humboldt Current. After several weeks in Guayaquil, Humboldt and his friends sailed for Acapulco, Mexico. Bonpland and Montúfar would return to South America—Bonpland eventually moved back to this botanist's paradise for good—but Humboldt would never set foot there again. Just as they were casting off for Mexico, the Cotopaxi volcano in Ecuador, which Humboldt had climbed only months before, erupted. Long after South America had diminished to a mere line on the horizon, Humboldt could hear the booming salute of the angry volcano.

The voyage to Acapulco took three months. "I arrived at Mexico by the South Sea in March 1803, and resided a year in that vast kingdom," Humboldt wrote. After the wonders of South America, Mexico was somewhat anticlimactic, but Humboldt's stay there was by no means unproductive. (Humboldt probably never lived an unproductive day in his entire adult life.) He would make no important scientific discoveries in Mexico, but his encyclopedic study of its history, economy, population, and geography would greatly expand European knowledge of

(continued on page 76)

The Hungry Gods

In March 1803, Alexander von Humboldt arrived in Mexico City, the capital of Mexico, where he intended to rest and recuperate from the effects of years of arduous travel and exploration in South America. As always, however, Humboldt's thirst for knowledge overcame his weariness, and his yearlong stay in Mexico bore little resemblance to a vacation. He spent much of his time involved in an exhaustive study of Mexico's history and the early civilizations— among them the Toltec and Aztec empires—that flourished in the Valley of Mexico from about 200 until the Spanish conquest in 1520.

Humboldt was particularly fascinated with the Aztec ("heron people") civilization, at its height from 1200 until 1520, when it was subdued and sent into decline by the Spanish conquistador Hernán Cortés. Several priceless Aztec codices (illustrated manuscripts) that Humboldt obtained opened doors onto that extraordinarily rich and multitextured culture, and throughout his year in Mexico he frequently could be seen, with codex in hand, prowling about the Aztec ruins of Tenochtitlán in Mexico City or examining other sites in and around the Valley of Mexico.

The Aztecs, Humboldt discovered, were a deeply spiritual people, and they practiced a complex religion featuring a multitude of deities. The Aztecs inherited many of their gods from the religions of Mexican civilizations that predated their own, and like the ancient Romans, the Aztecs also assimilated into their own religion the gods of those whom they subjugated. Among the Aztec pantheon were Tonatiuh, the sun god; Tezcatlipoca (smoking mirror), a god of wizardry and warfare; Tlaloc, a major fertility god; Tlazolteotl, the "eater of filth" to whom the Aztecs confessed their sins; and Quetzalcoatl, the winged serpent, a corn god.

The Aztec gods were fierce and demanding, and this gave rise to one of the most striking features of the Aztec religion—the practice of human sacrifice. Humboldt's codices provided him with chilling and graphic illustrations of this bloody ritual as practiced by the Aztecs. The sacrificial rites occurred in temples built atop great flat-topped pyramids. There, Aztec priests would cut the heart out of their living victim—usually a slave or prisoner of war—and offer the organ up to a certain god. (People who were sacrificed to the Aztec rain gods were drowned by the priests.) Some of the gods, represented by stone carvings that Humboldt described as "monstrous," were seemingly insatiable. According to one of his codices, 20,000 human sacrifices were made for the dedication of the pyramid and temple of Tenochtitlán.

The ruins of a great pyramid at Teotihuacán, located about 30 miles northeast of Mexico City and visited by Humboldt in 1803. Teotihuacán ("the place where the gods are") was built by a pre-Aztec society between A.D. *200 and 700.*

(continued from page 73)

this country, increasing in particular what Continentals knew of its ancient civilizations, such as those of the Aztec and Toltec, and its rich mineral resources.

Humboldt's first task was to find Acapulco—or at least to determine its exact location on Mexico's west coast, thus correcting a major error on the maps of his day (previously Acapulco had been depicted many miles too far to the east). Then, on a hot and dusty trip by horse and mule from Acapulco through the rugged Guerrero Mountains to Mexico City, Humboldt spent his days making notes on the geologic outcroppings he passed, and his nights searching for the familiar constellations he needed to determine the latitude and longitude of significant landmarks he encountered along his route.

Humboldt found the capital, Mexico City, to be a lovely if enormous metropolis—its population even then numbered around 6 million—of broad avenues and beautiful stone buildings of which, he wrote, "the balustrades and gates are all of Biscay iron, ornamented with bronze, and the houses, instead of roofs, have terraces like those in Italy and other southern cities." Here he spent seven months, devoting most of his time to research in governmental archives and at the city's school of mines. He also explored Aztec ruins on the Zócalo, Mexico City's main square; visited the ancient pyramids of Teotihuacán; and purchased a number of invaluable Aztec codices, which displayed "in every figure the extravagant imagination of a people who delighted to see the palpitating heart of human victims offered up to gigantic and monstrous idols."

From his base in Mexico City he also made a long jaunt to the province of Guanajuato, a mountainous region about 150 miles north of Mexico City. Humboldt spent an entire month visiting the local silver mines, the richest, he believed, in the New World. He collected so many mineral specimens that he had to hire a special mule train to carry them back to Mexico City. He and Bonpland then visited Jorullo, a volcano formed only 44 years earlier, in

Anthropology was one of the many disciplines that Humboldt contributed to during his lifetime. This bas-relief calendar, probably of Aztec origin, was one of the invaluable relics of ancient Mexican culture that Humboldt examined during his stay in Mexico City.

1759. Here Indians described for Humboldt the day their fields erupted in fire and a river evaporated into clouds of steam. Crossing still-smoldering lava fields, an enraptured Humboldt measured volcanic gases while Bonpland collected specimens of bizarre vegetation. Humboldt, to the amazement of the local Indians, climbed down into Jorullo's crater, where he made notes on the air and the volcano's hot springs.

In January 1804, Humboldt, Bonpland, and Montúfar left Mexico. Humboldt had been away from his home—and indeed, from his home continent—for five years. But he was still not quite ready to return to Europe and the comforts of Paris and Berlin. There was more to be done, new lands to visit and new information to be gathered and assimilated into the vast wealth of data he had already compiled. However, his newest goal was not a rain forest or a volcano or the ancient ruins of a vanished civilization; rather, Humboldt now hoped to explore one of the other great minds of his era. He was on his way to Washington, D.C., where he hoped to meet Thomas Jefferson of the United States.

A Premature Burial

Humboldt and his two fellow travelers arrived in Philadelphia in May 1804. Humboldt came ashore to find himself the darling of the American scientific community, which had learned of his South American exploits from European journals and newspapers. A seemingly endless round of dinners, teas, and testimonials began. The American Philosophical Society, the premier scientific association in the United States, immediately invited the Prussian to lecture and elected him a member. His fellow "philosophers" eagerly entertained him; he particularly enjoyed the company and hospitality of Caspar Wistar, a noted anatomist; Benjamin Smith Barton, a botanist and an expert on the American Indian; Benjamin Rush, a physician and a signer of the Declaration of Independence; and Charles Willson Peale, an artist who was famous for his portraits of George Washington and who owned Peale's Museum, noted not only for its zoological collection—which included the skeleton of a mammoth—but for its oddities, among them a stuffed five-legged, two-headed cow suckling a two-headed calf.

Humboldt accepted the attention gracefully; indeed, he basked in it, for he was a social creature by nature, loving good wine and good company, and his five years in the wilds of South America had left him starved for the pleasures of polite European society, even if it was actually once removed from Europe. The Americans, for their part, found that Humboldt was actually more impressive

Alexander von Humboldt emerged from the wilds of South America in December 1802.. News of his exploits—especially the ascent of Chimborazo—had already reached North America and Europe, and Humboldt arrived in Philadelphia, and then in Paris, to find that he was an international celebrity.

than his already considerable reputation had indicated. Brilliant and effortlessly witty in conversation, with the manners of an aristocrat but the heart and soul of a republican, a man who could brave the world's highest peaks and sketch, in detail, the most delicate of tropical flowers, a gentleman of noble birth who preached the gospel of abolitionism; surely, his hosts felt, this was a great personage.

The object of this admiration desired to meet someone he himself had long admired, and so, accompanied by Peale, Humboldt departed Philadelphia for Washington, D.C., where he was to be received by President Thomas Jefferson. Humboldt had written Jefferson as soon as he arrived in Philadelphia: "I feel it is my pleasant duty to present my respects and express my high admiration for your writings, your actions, and the liberalism of your ideas, which have inspired me from my earliest youth." Jefferson, being the president not only of the United States but also of the American Philosophical Society, knew of Humboldt and his discoveries and invited him to dinner at the executive mansion. The two men were quite taken with one another, and Jefferson invited Humboldt to Monticello, his plantation in Virginia, for an extended visit. They spent three weeks at Jefferson's estate, strolling and riding about the lovely countryside, endlessly discussing their mutual interests, which were many—paleontology, astronomy, meteorology, agriculture, philosophy, and, of course, politics. By the end of Humboldt's visit, a strong friendship had been forged, and although once Humboldt left America he never saw Jefferson again, the two men maintained a lifelong correspondence.

Finally, it was time for the great traveler to return to Europe and his own home. On June 30, 1804, Humboldt, Bonpland, and Montúfar sailed for France. Humboldt would never again visit the United States, but he remained fascinated with it until his death, following its progress

Charles Willson Peale, an artist and the curator of Peale's Museum in Philadelphia, entertained Humboldt during his visit to America. Peale's natural history museum had a wide selection of biological oddities, including stuffed two-headed animals.

and development through letters from American colleagues and newspaper reports. In turn, Americans retained a fascination with, and a great respect for, Humboldt. Especially after the publication of *Cosmos*, his last and greatest scientific treatise, Americans sought him out in Berlin. The esteem in which 19th-century Americans held him is reflected by the many places they named after him—Humboldt, Illinois; the town of Humboldt, in Humboldt County, Iowa; Humboldt County, Nevada; Humboldt Peak, in Colorado; Humboldt Bay, in Hum-

Humboldt returned to Paris in August 1804. Napoléon Bonaparte, emperor of France, seemed to be the only person in Paris who was not impressed by Humboldt; at their first and only encounter, Bonaparte insulted the scientist.

boldt County, California; and Humboldt State Park, in California, among others.

On August 1, 1804, *La Favorite*, the French ship that carried Humboldt, Bonpland, and Montúfar across the Atlantic, anchored off Bordeaux, France. Passengers and crew were quarantined for a few days—the final delay in a journey that had been plagued by delays—but they were eventually given clearance from French medical authorities to go ashore. Humboldt and Montúfar joyfully headed

for Paris, while Bonpland made for La Rochelle, where his brother lived.

Humboldt arrived in Paris only to learn that he was dead. In fact, according to various European periodicals, he had already died a number of deaths. Months after the actual climb took place, the French public had been enthralled by accounts of Humboldt's ascent of Chimborazo and then appalled when the papers mistakenly reported his death. A year before he returned home, a French newspaper announced that he had "perished among the savages of North America," and only a few weeks before his arrival in Europe the Hamburg *Correspondent* had run the following: "We regret to learn that the celebrated traveler, Herr von Humboldt, has been attacked with yellow fever, and has died at Acapulco." Humboldt himself accepted the news of his own demise with good humor; he was delighted by the idea that his fellow Prussians were mourning his death by "yellow fever" at a time when he was actually sipping wine at Thomas Jefferson's comfortable country estate. The rumors of his death, followed by his reappearance in the flesh, also helped to increase the considerable fame he had already acquired, and Humboldt arrived in Paris to find that he was, along with Napoléon himself, the most talked about man on the Continent.

The Parisians outdid the Philadelphians in honoring Humboldt. He was "feted all over town," according to his sister-in-law, and spent night after night in the salons of the high society French, where he told his stories time and time again. At the meetings of the many learned societies of Paris, then the cultural capital of the West, he captivated his colleagues. Two months after he arrived in Paris, Humboldt's public exhibit of his South American collections and drawings drew huge crowds. (There was apparently just one Parisian who resisted Humboldt's charms. When presented at the French court, Humboldt received but the briefest acknowledgement from Emperor

Napoléon Bonaparte, who had heard so much about Humboldt that he had become quite jealous. In fact, Napoléon openly belittled Humboldt, reportedly saying to him, "I understand you collect flowers. So does my wife.")

Humboldt found all the attention and accolades rewarding, and if he had so desired, he probably could have spent years dallying in salons and attending honorary banquets. But although his gut may have grown somewhat following his return to Europe, his ambition had not been dulled in the least. A truly gigantic task awaited him, a task that would prove to be even more exacting and challenging than his journeys through the rain forests of South America. It was of the utmost importance to Humboldt, and indeed to science, that he share what he had learned in South America, and he was not content to do so only informally, through word of mouth and show-and-tell. Although he spent some of the next 30 years in new pursuits, developing fresh scientific interests and playing diplomat for the Prussian crown, he devoted by far the greatest part of these years to the truly massive enterprise of putting his experiences and observations into book form and then publishing them.

Humboldt remained for as long as possible in Paris although soon after his return to Europe he made a short tour of Italy, which he followed with a stay of almost two years in his hometown of Berlin. But not until 1827 would he again establish a permanent residence in Berlin—and then only because the state of his finances had become so pitiful that he had to assume full-time duties as a court chancellor in order to receive a sufficient salary. In the interim he stayed in Paris, where he found the artists and engravers he needed to illustrate his books and the publishers he needed to print and distribute them. In Paris, Humboldt also had access to many other scientists—including Bonpland, who had once again joined him—and to the libraries he needed to help him interpret his data.

As always, he recognized the limits of his own knowledge and turned to specialists when necessary.

The data that Humboldt had collected was voluminous in every sense of the word. He had filled notebook after notebook with observations on magnetism, meteorology, climatology, geology, mineralogy, zoology, botany, plant geography, ethnography, and anthropology. He had studied linguistics and history. At sea he had dissected fish and measured the ocean's temperature and gravity. On the Orinoco he had calculated the altitude of the sun and the

Humboldt's diagram, entitled "Meso American Ruins," of an archaeological site in Mexico City where Aztec relics were being uncovered. Similar sketches and charts were featured in the public exhibits Humboldt gave in Paris during the autumn of 1804.

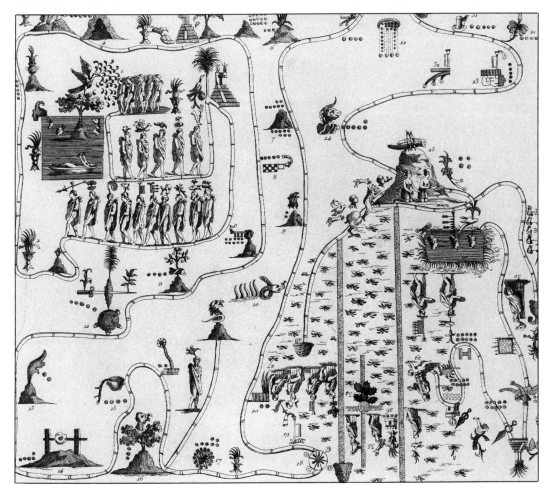

After his return to Europe, Humboldt dedicated most of his time to the task of publishing his books, but he never completely divorced himself from active scientific investigation and experimentation. Here, Humboldt (seated) and two colleagues are engaged in an experiment to determine the difference between the speed of light and the speed of sound.

stars and mapped the exact location of landmarks. He had made detailed sketches of monkeys and other animals and had recorded insect species. He had measured the temperature of the air, the earth, and the rivers. In the Andes he had analyzed the gases emitted by volcanoes and studied geology, collecting lava and pumice and sketching landforms. He had taken notes on a meteor shower in Venezuela and the passage of the planet Mercury across the face of the sun in Peru. Throughout South America, he had measured the dip of a magnetic needle, searching for the magnetic equator. He and Bonpland had collected over 60,000 plant specimens. In Mexico, Humboldt had purchased ancient manuscripts and sculptures. He had dispatched crates full of specimens of one sort or another to Europe throughout his travels, and he had boarded the ship for home with full cases. Initially, Humboldt planned to publish 11 volumes based on his New World observations; he expected this to take 2 or 3 years to accomplish. But he grossly underestimated both how much material he had to write up and how long it would take him to do so. He would wrestle with his manuscripts for more than 30 years, from 1804 to 1836, in the end publishing 30 volumes. The entire series he entitled *Voyages to the Equinoctial Regions of the New Continent, Made During the Years 1799 to 1804*. With characteristic generosity, he named Aimé Bonpland coauthor of the entire series, although Bonpland actually collaborated with him on only a few of the botany books. Most of the volumes first appeared in French (some were later translated into other languages), although Humboldt published two in German and one in Latin. Ten of the volumes were what publishers call quarto in size (small enough to fit easily in one's lap), and the other 20 were folio size (about the size of a large modern atlas). Altogether, *Voyages* included over 1,400 illustrations; the engravings cost Humboldt more than the entire South American expedition had, so inflating the series' price that few libraries and virtually no individual could afford to buy the entire set, although some single volumes sold very well.

Scientific treatises make up the bulk of the series, including two volumes coauthored by Humboldt and mathematician Jabbo Oltmanns. Consisting largely of astronomical tables, they are considerably less attractive and, at least to the general reader, less accessible than the two volumes on zoology Humboldt produced in collaboration with Baron Georges Cuvier, Pierre-André Latreille, and Achille Valenciennes. These texts describe in detail a wide variety of South American animal life, ranging from the crocodile to the tiniest of insects, some of which are illustrated in exquisite colored engravings.

The 11 volumes on botany that Humboldt wrote with the help of Bonpland and K. S. Kunth are even more elaborate. The texts catalog the South American flora, with entries describing the seeds, fruits, leaves, and other features of each plant. The botany catalogs include fabulously detailed engravings. Humboldt was the sole author of one of the most important volumes in the series, *Essay on the Geography of Plants*, published in 1807, which established a new branch of botany—plant geography. This volume contains one magnificent plate that illustrates Humboldt's essential botanical theorem: Scientists can predict which plants will grow in a given locale once they know that locale's altitude and mean temperature. To illustrate this, an engraving of a mountain shows the type of plants that grow at specific heights. Columns on the side expand on the idea, relating snow line, animal populations, and other factors relevant to plant geography.

Humboldt included in his series several volumes on history and geography that he hoped would capture the imagination of the general public. The most popular book he ever wrote, *Aspects of Nature*, appeared in 1807. In this book Humboldt devoted chapters to a variety of landscapes he had seen, including the forests of the Orinoco, the llanos, and the Andes. Neither a travel account nor a scientific treatise, *Aspects of Nature* was meant not only to inform but to inspire the reader, and it seems to have succeeded. In *Views of the Cordilleras*, published in 1814, the text is keyed to 69 enormous plates that depict South American landscapes and the remnants of the ancient Latin American civilizations, including manuscripts, art, and monuments. This book awakened serious scholarly interest in the Inca and Aztec cultures.

Also for the general public, Humboldt wrote a partial account of his expedition. First published in French and translated into English as *Personal Narrative* (first edition published in 1815), this book covers his time in Venezuela. The title is somewhat misleading, however; the book is written in a detached rather than a personal tone and is hardly a straightforward narrative of his adventures. In this massive work, which runs to six volumes and thousands of pages, Humboldt alternates between descriptions of his activities and dry comments on his scientific observations. Many pages consist almost totally of footnotes, referring the reader to the works of other scientists and explorers. Regrettably, Humboldt never published a personal account of his journeys through the Andes; for details of these years, scholars must turn to his letters.

In writing his *Political Essay on the Kingdom of New Spain* (published in 1811) and his *Political Essay on the Island of Cuba* (published in 1828) Humboldt founded the modern science of geography, relating the physical characteristics of these countries to their economic, social, and political features. Both books were of great interest to Europeans, who had been denied any information about the Spanish colonies. In fact, his geography of New Spain (Mexico), which contained a great deal of information about the Mexican mines, inspired many Europeans to invest in that nation after it won independence from Spain.

In all, Humboldt's publications on South America, Mexico, and Cuba represent a remarkable—indeed, an awe-inspiring —achievement. Even today many of the volumes are still read, especially by scholars of the history of science. And several are reprinted regularly. In fact, a reprint of the entire series has recently appeared, a fact that would surely have pleased Humboldt, for he spent not only 30 years of his life on them but the remainder of his personal fortune as well.

The Man Who Knew Everything

Absorbed as he was in his writing and publishing labors, the years passed quickly for Humboldt. When he was not holed up in his Berlin apartments (he had moved back to Berlin in 1827) working on a manuscript, he was seeing to his duties as the token liberal and "freethinker" at the court of the king of Prussia, Friedrich Wilhelm III. He traveled to France and England occasionally and was constantly in demand as a lecturer, for his reputation as a man of knowledge continued to grow as the years went by. One of his friends, the eminent German poet and dramatist Johann Wolfgang von Goethe, described the Humboldt of this period in a letter: "What a man he is! I have known him for so long, and yet he amazes me all over again. One can truly say that he has no equal in information and lively knowledge. He is everywhere at home and overwhelms one with intellectual treasures. He is like a fountain with many spouts at which one may simply fill one's pitchers—forever refreshing and unfailing."

And of course Humboldt did not neglect his social obligations; there remained in him throughout his life a part of that sickly little boy, confined to the house and yearning for friends. In addition to entertaining and being entertained in Berlin, London, Paris, Vienna, and elsewhere, Humboldt maintained a voluminous correspondence with associates around the world. In a single year he received

Following his return to Paris in 1804, Humboldt remained in Europe, spending most of his time in Paris or Berlin working on his manuscripts and attending the court of the king of Prussia. His exploring days were not quite over, however; in 1829, at the age of 60, he embarked on an expedition to Russia's Ural Mountains and beyond into central Asia.

close to 4,000 letters and wrote about 2,000. In December 1827, one letter in particular drew an immediate answer from Humboldt. Yegor Kankrin, Russia's finance minister, had written to extend to Humboldt an invitation to spend a summer exploring the Ural Mountains, which mark the boundary between Europe and Asia. Czar Nicholas I, eager to tap the rich mineral deposits found in the Urals, offered to underwrite the cost of Humboldt's tour. Humboldt, now 60 years old but as robust as ever—"I still walk very lightly on foot, nine to ten hours without resting, despite my age and my white hair," he wrote to Kankrin— did not have to be asked twice, for he had long harbored a wish to explore this little-known region.

Once again Humboldt found himself planning a major expedition, and he began considering whom he might choose to accompany him. The faithful Bonpland was gone, having vanished into the South American rain forests for good. (In 1814, in order to escape an unsuccessful marriage and to continue his botanical studies in the tropics, Bonpland had moved to Buenos Aires, Argentina. During a plant-collecting expedition into Paraguay, the botanist and his entourage were attacked by soldiers, who killed everybody except Bonpland. He was taken away in chains and pressed into medical service deep in the interior. Despite Humboldt's tireless efforts to secure his old friend's release, Bonpland was not given his freedom until 1830. Instead of returning to Europe, the disgusted Bonpland wandered off into the rain forest, where he lived out the rest of his days.) Humboldt chose two worthy scientists—Professor Christian Gottfried Ehrenberg, physician, biologist, and zoologist; and Gustav Rose, a chemist and mineralogist. Karl Seifert, Humboldt's valet, also came along; he would attend to the baggage, an important responsibility.

Winter still lingered in Eastern Europe when the Humboldt party set out from Berlin on April 12, 1829. Unlike

on the South American journeys, Humboldt would not have to do much walking this time; the czar had outfitted the party with horses and carriages, in which the three scientists rode, bundled up in heavy coats and layers of blankets. Despite such luxuries, it was rough going. Heading north along the Baltic Sea, the carriages moved slowly through snowstorms and sleet. Ice made the roads treacherous, and thaws sometimes created such deep mud that Humboldt had to hire a second team of horses, or a team of peasants, to pull the carriages through. The rivers the party encountered were swollen and frequently ice laden, and crossing them with rafts and sailboats was a harrowing experience. Once they spent several days waiting for drift

Humboldt's Urals expedition arrived in the Russian city of St. Petersburg on May 1, 1829. Humboldt discovered that even here his name was well known and that Russian scientists were quite familiar with his writings.

ice to break up so that they could cross a lagoon. Humboldt, as usual, put the delays to good use, measuring the earth's magnetic intensity whenever he could.

At other times, however, Humboldt's journey through Eastern Europe seemed more like the progression of a royal caravan than a scientific expedition. Mounted couriers came and went with messages, salutations, and invitations from the czar and other Russian dignitaries. At Tartu, Estonia, Humboldt was subjected, in his own words, to "professorial visits from 8 o'clock in the morning until 9 o'clock at night, and a splendid dinner given by the whole university with obbligato toasts." And in Riga, they were "met by a mail courier who rides in front now and gives

As Humboldt's expedition drew closer to the Urals, the landscape became increasingly inhospitable and roads virtually nonexistent. Lumbermen, trappers, and political criminals on their way to Siberian exile peopled the countryside.

us such a prosperous air that we have to pay 60 to 70 shillings for [lodgings for] one night." They received an even grander reception when, on May 1, they finally arrived in the great city of St. Petersburg, located in northwestern Russia close to the Finnish border. There, Humboldt dined almost daily with the czar and his family. "Everywhere I go," he wrote, "they offer me money like hay and anticipate my every wish."

From St. Petersburg they set off for the Urals, situated about 1,200 miles, as the crow flies, to the southeast. The party was swelling rapidly with Russian mining officials, scientists, and bureaucrats. Previously, the travelers had required only six or eight horses at a time. Now so many carriages accompanied them that 30 or 40 horses might be hired at a stop. Beyond Moscow they found few hotels or inns, and some nights were spent in postal stations. Others were spent on the estates of wealthy families. While they were on the road, Humboldt drove the horses relentlessly; the oncoming warm weather would last only a short time, and he wished to be back in St. Petersburg before the brutal Russian winter returned.

By June 1 they had reached Nizhni Novgorod (now known as Gorki), a city located on the Volga River about midway between St. Petersburg and the Urals. Here, they drove their carriages onto a big barge, which was outfitted with a table and benches and a brick stove, all protected by an awning. A raft carrying provisions was towed behind. Four boatmen, chanting mournful dirges, poled the barge eastward along the swollen Volga for 200 miles. On June 4 the party disembarked at Kazan, a large city whose population of Tatars and Oriental architecture gave it an Eastern atmosphere. From Kazan, the party set out on the final, 500-mile push to the Urals. The countryside grew less hospitable, and at night they often slept in their carriages. By day they passed ragged gangs of criminals and political prisoners walking toward exile in the endless, frozen plains of Siberia.

They arrived at Ekaterinburg (now known as Sverd-lovsk), a town in the central Urals, on June 15. Humboldt gladly quit his carriage; he would have little use for it during the next month. With Ekaterinburg as a base, Humboldt hiked out to study nearby mines and mineral deposits. He collected specimens of iron, copper, mala-chite, beryl, topaz, gold, and platinum. In St. Petersburg, he had told the czar that he expected to find diamonds in the Urals. None had ever been discovered outside the tropics, but Humboldt believed that Russia's geology was similar to Brazil's, where diamonds were found in gold-bearing rivers. En route to the Urals, Humboldt had dis-cussed this with a nobleman whose mountain estate in-cluded rivers that yielded gold. Arriving at his home, the count ordered his miners to search the riverbeds, and within days he was rewarded with the discovery of a dia-mond. (After he had returned to Berlin, Humboldt himself received a large diamond in the mail from the grateful count.)

From the Urals the party struck out across the steppes of Siberia for the Altai Mountains, which are located 1,000 miles from Ekaterinburg, on the Russian border with China and Mongolia. Humboldt had imagined the Si-berian flatlands to be brown and dry but found them well watered with lush, low vegetation. Of animals he could say little, seeing almost none, although he did hear of tigers in Siberia. Halting only occasionally now for Hum-boldt to make astronomical observations, the party covered huge stretches of land each day. "One travels—or rather flees—over these monotonous grasslands," Humboldt wrote, "sailing on land as it were, in which we covered 140 miles in twenty-four hours." Gigantic mosquitoes be-gan to plague them; Humboldt declared that they were nastier than any of the mosquitoes he had encountered in South America. The travelers resorted to wearing heavy leather caps with horsehair veils, which proved to be ter-ribly uncomfortable. The weather made them miserable as well. The temperature registered 85 degrees in the shade during the day but fell to 36 degrees at night.

On August 1, at two o'clock in the morning, they arrived at the town of Barnaul in the Altai Mountains, but only after waiting for hours to cross the Ob River; a gale had so raged that the Ob "had waves like the sea." From Barnaul they traveled another 300 miles southeast, along the Upper Irtysh River and through Cossack villages, until they reached the Russian-Chinese border. Here, having penetrated 1,000 miles into central Asia, they came to a stop at a Chinese frontier outpost manned by a Chinese border official in a blue silk robe with peacock feathers in his pointed cap. Gifts were exchanged. Here, their journey came to an end, and they began to prepare for the return trip. Before they departed, Humboldt and Rose climbed a nearby hill to take a final look around. For the last time

In the heat of July and August the Humboldt party traveled 1,000 miles across the vast, grassy steppes that lay between the Ural and Altai mountain ranges. Penetrating deep into central Asia, they frequently encountered nomadic Mongolian herdsmen and their flocks.

Humboldt's route ----

Humboldt's Russian Expedition

Humboldt's central Asian expedition began in Riga, passed through the Russian cities of St. Petersburg, Moscow, and Gorki (Nizhni Novgorod), sailed up the Volga River to Kazan, and from there traveled overland to Sverdlovsk (Ekaterinburg) in the Urals. Humboldt then crossed the Siberian steppes to Barnaul in the Altai Mountains, and the expedition came to an end near Lake Zaysan Nor (Lake Zaisan).

in his life, Humboldt was surrounded by the unlimited horizons and unknown lands that had called to him since he was a child in Prussia. He could see the vast steppes leading up to distant, snowy mountain ranges; Lake Zaisan shimmered in the sun; and to the south lay the great and mysterious Gobi Desert. How Humboldt longed to continue southward to discover the secrets of that strange ecosystem! The other members of the expedition had been on their horses or in their carriages for a long time before Humboldt came down and joined them. They were back in Moscow by November.

By the time Humboldt, Rose, Ehrenberg, and Seifert returned to Berlin in late December they had traveled

almost 12,000 miles. Overall, Humboldt expressed considerable satisfaction with the expedition. Rose published
an account of their travels and their mineralogical and
geologic discoveries, and Humboldt himself published
three volumes of *Central Asia*, which appeared in 1843.
The first two volumes described what he had learned of
the Asian mountain ranges in Russia and farther east (he
based the Himalayan section on information he obtained
from Asian merchants). The third volume covered his
magnetic and climatological observations. But Humboldt
took the greatest pride in the magnetic and meteorological
observation stations that the Russian government set up
across European and Asian Russia in response to his rec-
ommendations. Later, Humboldt persuaded the British to
establish similar stations in their colonies; eventually, such
stations ringed the globe and represented one of the first
examples of international scientific collaboration. Scientific collaboration, and indeed collaboration of any kind,
was a concept that was very close to Humboldt's heart.

Humboldt's central Asian expedition also swelled the
explorer's fame to unprecedented proportions, and de-
servedly so, for he was an unprecedented figure. An amusing incident that occurred toward the end of the journey
is indicative of the scope of Humboldt's reputation. As the
caravan was making its way across the western Siberian
steppes, a local Mongolian herdsman appeared and ac-
costed Humboldt, who, although he could not understand
a word of the harangue, listened politely. "What does this
gentleman want?" Humboldt finally asked. An interpreter
was found. He explained that several of the herdsman's
horses had been stolen. The Mongolian, hearing that a
great man—a man who knew everything—was passing
through the area, had come to Humboldt to ask him where
the stolen horses were. It would not have been surprising
if Humboldt had given the herdsman an answer to his
question.

Cosmos

I have the crazy notion to depict the entire material universe, all that we know of the phenomena of universe and earth, from spiral nebulae to the geography of mosses and granite rocks, in one work—and in a vivid language that will stimulate and elicit feeling. Every great and important idea that glows in my writing should here be registered side by side with facts. It should portray an epoch in the spiritual genesis of mankind—in the knowledge of nature. But it is not to be taken as a physical description of earth: it comprises heaven and earth, the whole of creation."

With these words, in 1834 Alexander von Humboldt announced to his friend Karl August Varnhagen von Ense, a prominent historian and biographer, his plan to begin the writing of *Cosmos*, the volume that was to stand as the crowning achievement of a remarkable career. Although he was in his sixties, Humboldt had lost none of the drive that had propelled him thus far. Nor had he lost any of his vaulting ambition; *Cosmos*, which he called "the most important work of my life," was to be no less than an attempt to describe and explain the entire universe as 19th-century man knew it and, just as importantly, to enlighten the average reader to the "unity in the vast diversity of phenomena." At a dinner given in honor of Humboldt in Moscow following the expedition to the Urals, a speaker had eulogized him as the "Prometheus of our days." Now Humboldt was indeed assuming the

In the years following his expedition to central Asia, Humboldt enjoyed his reputation as the most learned man in Europe, and he did nothing that might have caused his contemporaries to see him in a less flattering light. The publication of the first volume of Cosmos, in 1845, was final proof that Humboldt's intellect was one of the most brilliant of the 19th century.

Humboldt's celebrity status had some drawbacks. King Friedrich Wilhelm III of Prussia, for example, expected him to spend his days and nights serving the royal court as host, entertainer, and wise man.

role of the bringer of light—the light and illumination of knowledge.

Like Humboldt's other great endeavor—the exploration of South America—the writing of *Cosmos* was constantly delayed by obstacles of one kind or another. During the South American expeditions, Humboldt had been beset by storms and shipwrecks, jaguars and electric eels, typhoid and malaria. In Europe, as he tried to write *Cosmos*, he was confronted with obstacles of a more civilized—but no less troublesome—nature. As privy councillor and roving diplomat for Friedrich Wilhelm III, he was obliged to travel extensively. These European journeys were tiresome and time-consuming. And when Humboldt was not on the road, the king required him to perform as a kind of court sage, educator, and entertainer all rolled into one. These duties were even more irksome than the diplomatic jaunts, for the king demanded advice from Humboldt on all possible subjects, be they philosophical, scientific, social, political, personal, or whatever. In the evenings, he was expected to entertain and educate the royal family by reading aloud and discoursing on art and science. Even the death of Friedrich Wilhelm III did not release Humboldt; his services were immediately retained by the successor to the throne, Friedrich Wilhelm IV. This, perhaps, was the price to be paid for being known as the most learned man in the world. Only in 1858, when Friedrich Wilhelm IV lost his mind and the regency was passed to his younger brother, did Humboldt, then 88, leave the court circle.

But Humboldt proved—as he had in South America— to be endlessly resourceful in overcoming all the things that stood in the way of his *Cosmos* project. He was ingenious in finding ways to avoid his court duties, and when he could not sidestep them, he compensated; even in his seventies and eighties he displayed almost superhuman powers of concentration, discipline, and physical stamina.

Often, he would return from court duties late in the evening and then work until dawn on his manuscript. In this manner he spent the final 30 years of his life, racing against time to finish his great work.

The first volume of *Cosmos* appeared in 1845, and the second volume was published two years later. The overwhelming public response to the work proved that Humboldt had succeeded in his goal to "stimulate and elicit feeling" from the average reader. Humboldt's publisher described the reaction to *Cosmos*: "In the history of book-publishing the demand is epoch-making. Book parcels destined for London and Saint Petersburg were torn out of our hands by agents who wanted their orders filled for the

Humboldt at home in his personal cosmos, his apartment in Berlin, where he worked ceaselessly on Cosmos *until his death, at the age of 89, in 1859.*

bookstores in Vienna and Hamburg. Regular battles were fought over possession of this edition, and bribes offered for priorities. . . . This race by booksellers, unheard-of since the first editions of Schiller and Goethe . . . is overwhelming proof of a demonstrative desire of the public to read . . . your immortal work."

Humboldt, the bringer of light, had succeeded, if only for a moment, in illuminating for his fellow humans the awesome and sublime nature of the universe they inhabited and their spiritual as well as physical relationship with it. "Whether in the Amazonian forests or on the ridge of the high Andes," he wrote, "I was ever aware that *one* breath, from pole to pole, breathes *one* single life into rocks, plants, and the swelling breast of man." How timely is Humboldt's message for today's world, as our rain forests are ravaged, our wildlife is pushed to the brink of extinction, and the very atmosphere is befouled, for nobody understood better than he that to destroy our planet is to destroy ourselves.

Even after the publication of the first two volumes of *Cosmos*, Humboldt did not rest; there was more, so much more to write about. He worked feverishly on the third volume of *Cosmos*, but he died, on May 6, 1859, at the age of 89, before he could finish it. Many considered this a tragedy, but in retrospect it is clear that *Cosmos* would have continued to grow for as long as Humboldt continued to live, for he was a man who never rested on past achievements, who never became self-satisfied, and who remained hungry for new knowledge until his dying day.

A New York *Tribune* reporter went to Berlin to interview Humboldt shortly before the great man's death. There, in a "plain, two storey house, with a dull pink front," the reporter was invited into a room "filled with stuffed birds and other objects of natural history." Tables were heaped with letters, maps, manuscripts, and folios. "Humboldt immediately appeared," the reporter wrote. "He came up to me with a heartiness and cordiality which made me feel

Alexander von Humboldt, world traveler, finally came to rest at Schloss Tegel; the gentle Brandenburg countryside had been the scene of his first journeys of discovery, and from there he departed on his last.

that I was in the presence of a friend." The reporter was struck by the physical appearance of the scientist: "The first impression made by Humboldt's face was that of a broad and genial humanity. A pair of clear blue eyes, as bright and steady as a child's, met your own. His wrinkles were few and small, and his skin had a smoothness and delicacy rarely seen in old men. His hair, although snow white, was still abundant, his step slow but firm, and his manner active almost to the point of restlessness." Shortly before parting company with Humboldt, the reporter noticed a live chameleon in a glass terrarium. "He can turn one eye towards heaven, while with the other he inspects the earth," Humboldt remarked playfully—a description that suited himself as well as the lizard.

Further Reading

Baker, J. N. L. A *History of Geographical Discovery and Exploration*. New York: Cooper Square, 1967.

Botting, Douglas. *Humboldt and the Cosmos*. New York: Harper & Row, 1973.

Bowen, Margaret. *Empiricism and Geographical Thought: From Francis Bacon to Alexander von Humboldt*. Cambridge, England: Cambridge University Press, 1981.

Gillespie, Charles Coulston, ed. *Dictionary of Scientific Biography*. New York: Scribners, 1970–76.

Goetzmann, William H. *New Lands, New Men: America and the Second Great Age of Discovery*. New York: Viking, 1986.

Goulding, Michael. *The Fishes and the Forest: Explorations in Amazonian Natural History*. Berkeley: University of California Press, 1981.

Hegen, Edmund E. *Highways into the Upper Amazon Basin: Pioneer Lands in Southern Colombia, Ecuador & Northern Peru*. Gainesville: University Presses of Florida, 1967.

Houghton, Lord. *Monographs Personal and Social*. Reprint of 1873 edition. Philadelphia: Richard West, 1973.

Humboldt, Alexander von. *Aspects of Nature, in different Lands and Different Climates; with Scientific Elucidations*. London: Longman, 1850.

———. *Political Essay on the Kingdom of New Spain*. Reprint of 1811 edition. New York: AMS Press, 1966.

———. *Voyages to the Equinoctial Regions of the New Continent, Made During the Years 1799–1804*. London: Longman, 1814–29.

Kellner, L. *Alexander von Humboldt*. London: Oxford University Press, 1963.

O'Hanlon, Redmond. *In Trouble Again: A Journey Between the Orinoco and the Amazon*. New York: Atlantic Monthly Press, 1989.

Terra, Helmut de. *The Life and Times of Alexander von Humboldt: 1769–1859*. New York: Knopf, 1955.

Chronology

Entries in roman type refer to events directly related to exploration and Humboldt's life; entries in italics refer to important historical and cultural events of the time.

1500	Alonso de Ojeda and Amerigo Vespucci discover the mouth of the Amazon River
1513	Vasco Núñez de Balboa crosses the Isthmus of Panama and discovers the Pacific Ocean
1541	Francisco de Orellana descends the Amazon River
Sept. 14, 1769	Friedrich Wilhelm Karl Heinrich Alexander von Humboldt born in Berlin, in the kingdom of Prussia
1770	Captain James Cook discovers Botany Bay, Australia
1775	*American Revolution begins*
1789	*French Revolution begins*; Humboldt enrolls at the University of Göttingen
1791	Humboldt enrolls at the Freiberg College of Mining
1796–1815	*Napoleonic Wars in Europe*
1800	Humboldt and his partner, Aimé Bonpland, explore the Orinoco and Apure rivers; they collect thousands of plant and animal specimens; Humboldt fills volumes of notebooks with scientific observations and charts
1802	Ascends to 19,280 feet on Chimborazo, a dormant volcano, attaining the highest altitude yet recorded by humans; explores Peru, Ecuador, and Mexico

1803   Travels in the United States, where he meets President Thomas Jefferson and is accorded celebrity status

1804   Returns to Europe

1805   First volume of *Voyages to the Equinoctial Regions of the New Continent, Made During the Years 1799–1804* is published; the series will conclude in 1836 after 30 volumes are completed

1808   *Goethe completes first part of* Faust

1811   *Political Essay on the Kingdom of New Spain*, with A *Political Essay on the Island of Cuba*, is published; Humboldt introduces the science of modern geography

1817–21   *Argentina, Chile, Peru, Guatemala, Panama, and Santo Domingo all proclaim their independence from Spain*

1827   Humboldt invited by Russian finance minister Yegor Kankrin to explore the Ural Mountains

1828   Signs contract with a German publisher to produce *Cosmos*; spends the better part of his last 30 years devoted to the task

April–Dec. 1829   Sets out with traveling party from Berlin across the Urals to Siberia and back again

1830   Sent by Friedrich Wilhelm III to establish contact with new government of Louis Philippe in France

1845   The first volume of *Cosmos* appears

May 6, 1859   Humboldt dies at the age of 89

Index

Picture Credits

Ann Gaines, a resident of San Antonio, has a master's degree in American civilization from the University of Texas at Austin. She has written extensively about the exploration of the Americas.

William H. Goetzmann holds the Jack S. Blanton, Sr., Chair in History at the University of Texas at Austin, where he has taught for many years. The author of numerous works on American history and exploration, he won the 1967 Pulitzer and Parkman prizes for his *Exploration and Empire: The Role of the Explorer and Scientist in the Winning of the American West, 1800–1900.* With his son William N. Goetzmann, he coauthored *The West of the Imagination,* which received the Carr P. Collins Award in 1986 from the Texas Institute of Letters. His documentary television series of the same name received a blue ribbon in the history category at the American Film and Video Festival held in New York City in 1987. A recent work, *New Lands, New Men: America and the Second Great Age of Discovery,* was published in 1986 to much critical acclaim.

Michael Collins served as command module pilot on the *Apollo 11* space mission, which landed his colleagues Neil Armstrong and Buzz Aldrin on the moon. A graduate of the United States Military Academy, Collins was named an astronaut in 1963. In 1966 he piloted the *Gemini 10* mission, during which he became the third American to walk in space. The author of several books on space exploration, Collins was director of the Smithsonian Institution's National Air and Space Museum from 1971 to 1978 and is a recipient of the Presidential Medal of Freedom.